THE 2008 CHARLTON COIN GUIDE

47th EDITION

Dealer's buying prices for
Canadian, Newfoundland and Maritime coinage,
Canadian Medals, Tokens and Paper Money,
United States and World Gold Coinage

by
W. K. Cross

The Charlton Press

Toronto, Ontario • Palm Harbor, Florida

Library and Archives Canada Cataloguing this publication as follows

Charlton, J.E., 1911
Charlton coin guide

18th- ed.; 1978--
Continues: CharltonJ.E., 1911- Coin guide of Canadian, Newfoundland and Maritime coinage, ISSN 0701-8223.
ISSN 0706-0459
ISBN 978-0-88968-325-9 (47th edition)

1. Coins, Canadian–Periodicals. 2. Coins, Canadian--Priices--Periodicals
I. Title.

CJ1864.C5114 18- 1978- 737.4'9'71 C79-030323-X

Printed in Canada
in the Province of Quebec

The Charlton Press

Post Office Box 820, Station Willowdale B
North York, Ontario. M2K 2R1 Canada
Tel: 416-488-1418 Fax: 416-488-4656
Tel: 800-442-6042 Fax: 800-442-1542
www.charltonpress.com; E-mail: chpress@charltonpress.com

CONTENTS

INDEX OF DEALERS

Note: Prices in this book are based on gold and silver values as of July 18th, 2007, and Canadian / United States foreign currency rates of the same day.

INTRODUCTION

It is more difficult to obtain old coins in circulation, much more so than it was twenty-five years ago. For the most part silver no longer circulates, since its bullion value now exceeds its face value. Generally speaking, the only pre-1968 coins in circulation are one-cent and five-cent pieces, and these seldom pre-date 1953. Older coins must now be purchased through dealers.

BUYING AND SELLING PRICES

Buying prices are what dealers pay for coins. Selling prices are what dealers charge for coins. Generally, dealers will pay 40% to 60% of their selling price. It should be remembered all dealers will pay according to their needs. They will pay well for what they need immediately, but for those coins for which there is no demand, even if they have a high retail value, they will offer substantially less.

The prices shown in this book represent averages or estimates of buying prices and should serve as a guide in negotiating fair prices when buying or selling. Also a clearer idea of which coins are in demand by collectors and dealers can be developed by studying the guide.

Coins should not be mailed for appraisal unless a written response to an inquiry is received from the dealer. If coins are mailed, then they should be sent by registered mail, insured, accompanied by a list of the coins sent, with a complete return address and return postage.

HANDLING AND CLEANING COINS

Coins should be handled by the edges only. Avoid touching the surfaces. Many collectors have found too late that fingerprints cannot be removed from coins or other metal valuables. Proof and specimen quality coins must be handled with extra care since their high lustre is very fragile.

Inevitably, the question of whether to clean coins or not will arise. Probably the best course to follow is, when in doubt don't, until you have contacted an experienced collector or dealer.

The tarnish on silver coins can be removed, but it will not necessarily raise the value. If the tarnish is very thick, then its removal could leave the coin looking much worse.

Nickel coins seldom require cleaning, and only soap and water are safe since nickel is a fairly active metal. Copper and bronze should not be cleaned by anyone who is not knowledgeable in the chemical properties of these metals and their alloys.

Whatever the metal, abrasives must never be used. There are many polishes on the market which are designed for silverware, copper and brass. These must not be used with coins. The results are disastrous.

HANDLING AND CLEANING PAPER MONEY

Inexperienced collectors should always use great care when handling notes. Notes should be handled as little as possible, since oil and perspiration from one's skin can damage and devalue a note. Care should be taken to ensure that unfolded or uncreased notes remain so, and that even marginal tears or abrasions are avoided. Under no circumstances should one ever wash or otherwise try to clean a note since it is likely that the note's value will be considerably reduced. The same is true for ironing or pressing. It should be avoided.

MINT MARKS

A mint mark is a letter stamped on a coin to designate the mint that produced the coins.

Canadian decimal coinage issued prior to 1908 was struck at either the Tower Mint, London, in which case it has no mint mark, or at the Heaton Mint in Birmingham. The Birmingham coins have a small "H" as a mint mark. Since 1908 all Canadian coins have been struck at the Ottawa or Winnipeg Mints, with no mint marks, except the Canadian sovereigns which were identified by a small "C" above the date and a "W" when struck at Winnipeg.

Newfoundland's coinage was struck at either London, Birmingham, or Ottawa. The Tower Mint coins had no marks, the Birmingham coins had an "H," and the Ottawa coins had a "C," except for the 1940 and 1942 cent pieces.

The coinage of New Brunswick and Nova Scotia had no mint marks because it was struck at the Tower Mint. Prince Edward Island's coinage was struck at Birmingham, but no mint mark was used because the dies were supplied by the Tower Mint.

COMPOSITION MARKS

Beginning in 1999, the Royal Canadian Mint, after years of development began issuing multiply plated steel coinage. Coins made by this new method carry the letter "P", for plated, on the obverse below the Queen's portrait.

ROYAL CANADIAN MINT LOGO

Beginning in 2006 the "P" composition mark was replaced by the Royal Canadian Mint logo.

COINS OF CANADA

NOVA SCOTIA

VICTORIA 1861 - 1864

Date and Denomination	Buying Price
1861 half cent	2.50
1864 half cent	2.50
1861 one cent	1.75
1862 one cent	25.00
1864 one cent	1.75

PRINCE EDWARD ISLAND

VICTORIA 1871

Date and Denomination	Buying Price
1871 one cent	1.75

NEW BRUNSWICK

VICTORIA 1861 - 1864

Date and Denomination	Buying Price
1861 half cent	75.00
1861 one cent	2.00
1864 one cent	2.00
1862 five cents	30.00
1864 five cents	30.00
1862 ten cents	35.00
1864 ten cents	45.00
1862 twenty cents	14.00
1864 twenty cents	17.50

IMPORTANT: Buying prices are listed for coins graded VG or better. Bent, damaged or badly worn coins are not collectable and bring no premium value.

NEWFOUNDLAND

LARGE CENTS

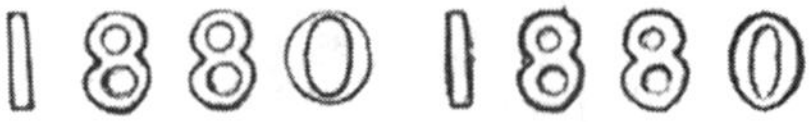

Wide 0　　　　Narrow 0

VICTORIA 1865 - 1896

Date and Mint Mark	Description	Buying Price
1865		2.00
1872H		1.75
1873		2.00
1876H		2.00
1880	Wide 0	1.75
1880	Narrow 0	70.00
1885		15.00
1888		15.00
1890		1.75
1894		1.75
1896		1.75

EDWARD VII 1904 - 1909

Date and Mint Mark	Buying Price
1904H	3.00
1907	1.25
1909	1.25

GEORGE V 1913 - 1936

Date and Mint Mark	Buying Price
1913	.50
1917C	.50
1919C	.50
1920C	.50
1929	.50
1936	.50

SMALL CENTS

GEORGE VI 1938 - 1947

Date and Mint Mark	Description	Buying Price
1938		.20
1940		.65
1940	Re-engraved Date	15.00
1941C		.20
1942		.15
1943C		.15
1944C		.60
1947C		.20

FIVE CENTS

VICTORIA 1865 - 1880

Date and Mint Mark	Buying Price
1865	20.00
1870	30.00
1872H	30.00
1873	60.00
1873H	400.00
1876H	85.00
1880	30.00

VICTORIA 1881 - 1896

Date and Mint Mark	Buying Price
1881	25.00
1882H	14.00
1885	85.00
1888	25.00
1890	6.00
1894	5.00
1896	3.00

EDWARD VII 1903 - 1908

Date and Mint Mark	Buying Price
1903	3.00
1904H	1.50
1908	1.75

GEORGE V 1912 - 1929

Date and Mint Mark	Buying Price
1912	1.00
1917C	1.00
1919C	2.25
1929	1.00

GEORGE VI 1938 - 1947

Date and Mint Mark	Buying Price
1938	.60
1940C	.60
1941C	.60
1942C	.60
1943C	.60
1944C	.60
1945C	.60
1946C	150.00
1947C	.60

TEN CENTS

VICTORIA 1865 - 1896

Date and Mint Mark	Buying Price
1865	17.50
1870	100.00
1872H	10.00
1873	20.00
1876H	25.00
1880	30.00
1882H	20.00
1885	70.00
1888	30.00
1890	5.00
1894	5.00
1896	5.00

EDWARD VII 1903 - 1904

Date and Mint Mark	Buying Price
1903	5.00
1904H	2.00

GEORGE V 1912 -1919

Date and Mint Mark	Buying Price
1912	.75
1917C	.75
1919C	.75

IMPORTANT: Buying prices are listed for coins graded VG or better. Bent, damaged or badly worn coins are not collectable and bring no premium value.

GEORGE VI 1938 - 1947

Date and Mint Mark	Buying Price
1938	.65
1940	.65
1941C	.65
1942C	.65
1943C	.65
1944C	.65
1945C	.55
1946C	1.00
1947C	.55

TWENTY CENTS

VICTORIA 1865 - 1900

Date and Mint Mark	Buying Price
1865	8.50
1870	12.00
1872H	7.00
1873	13.00
1876H	13.00
1880	15.00
1881	8.00
1882H	5.00
1885	8.00
1888	5.00
1890	5.00
1894	5.00
1896	5.00
1899	3.00
1900	3.00

EDWARD VII 1904

Date and Mint Mark	Buying Price
1904H	8.00

GEORGE V 1912

Date and Mint Mark	Buying Price
1912	1.00

TWENTY-FIVE CENTS

GEORGE V 1917 - 1919

Date and Mint Mark	Buying Price
1917C	1.30
1919C	1.30

IMPORTANT: A mint mark is a letter stamped on a coin to designate the mint that produced the coin. The Canadian Mint used the letter "C" or "W," while the Heaton Mint in England used the letter "H."

IMPORTANT: Buying prices listed are for coins graded VG or better. Bent, damaged or badly worn coins are not collectable and bring no premium over the silver value.

FIFTY CENTS

VICTORIA 1870 - 1900

Date and Mint Mark	Buying Price
1870	10.00
1872H	8.00
1873	30.00
1874	15.00
1876H	20.00
1880	16.00
1881	12.00
1882H	8.00
1885	16.00
1888	25.00
1894	7.00
1896	5.00
1898	5.00
1899	5.00
1900	5.00

EDWARD VII 1904 - 1909

Date and Mint Mark	Buying Price
1904H	3.00
1907	3.00
1908	3.00
1909	3.00

GEORGE V 1911 - 1919

Date and Mint Mark	Buying Price
1911	3.00
1917C	3.00
1918C	3.00
1919C	3.00

TWO DOLLARS GOLD

VICTORIA 1865 - 1888

Date and Mint Mark	Buying Price
1865	125.00
1870	125.00
1872	150.00
1880	600.00
1881	100.00
1882H	100.00
1885	100.00
1888	95.00

Note: Two dollar gold coins must be VF condition or better. Damaged, bent or holed coins are bought for gold content.

PROVINCE OF CANADA

LARGE CENTS

Wide 9 over 8 | Narrow 9

VICTORIA 1858 - 1859

Date and Mint Mark	Description	Buying Price
1858		45.00
1859	Narrow 9	3.00
1859	* Brass N9	2,500.00
1859	W/9 over 8	25.00

FIVE CENTS

Large date | Small date

VICTORIA 1858

Date and Mint Mark	Description	Buying Price
1858	Small Date	12.50
1858	Large Date	100.00

TEN CENTS

VICTORIA 1858

Date and Mint Mark	Buying Price
1858	15.00
1858 8/5	500.00

Note: * Brass metal is yellow in colour.

TWENTY CENTS

VICTORIA 1858

Date and Mint Mark	Buying Price
1858	35.00

CANADA

LARGE CENTS

Small date Small leaves

Large date Large leaves

VICTORIA 1876 - 1901

Date and Mint Mark	Description	Buying Price
1876H		2.00
1881H		3.50
1882H		3.50
1884		2.50
1886		4.00
1887		2.50
1888		2.50
1890H		5.00
1891	Large Leaves, Large Date	5.00
1891	Large Leaves, Small Date	50.00
1891	Small Leaves, Small Date	35.00
1892		4.00
1893		2.00
1894		7.50
1895		4.00
1896		2.50
1897		2.50
1898H		5.00
1899		2.50
1900		5.00
1900H		2.00
1901		2.00

EDWARD VII 1902 - 1910

Date and Mint Mark	Buying Price
1902	1.00
1903	1.00
1904	1.25
1905	1.25
1906	1.25
1907	1.25
1907H	5.00
1908	1.25
1909	1.00
1910	1.00

GEORGE V 1911 - 1920

Date and Mint Mark	Buying Price
1911	.65
1912	.65
1913	.65
1914	.65
1915	.30
1916	.30
1917	.30
1918	30
1919	.30
1920	.30

SMALL CENTS

1936 Dot

GEORGE V 1920 - 1936

Date and Mint Mark	Description	Buying Price
1920		.05
1921		.05
1922		7.00
1923		10.00
1924		3.00
1925		10.00
1926		1.25
1927		.05
1928		.05
1929		.05
1930		1.00
1931		.10
1932		.05
1933		.05
1934		.05
1935		.05
1936		.05
1936	Dot	50,000.00

Note: The 1936 Dot one cent coin is very rare, only four are confirmed. Examples must be authenticated and certified as counterfiet examples do exist.

1947 Maple Leaf
Blunt 7

1947 Maple Leaf
Pointed 7

GEORGE VI 1937 - 1947

Date and Mint Mark	Description	Buying Price
1937 to 1947		.01
1947	Maple Leaf, Blunt 7	1.00
1947	Maple Leaf, Pointed 7	.01

"A" points
to denticles

"A" points
between denticles

GEORGE VI 1948 - 1952

Date and Mint Mark	Description	Buying Price
1948	"A" Points to	.01
1948	"A" Between	.10
1949	"A" Points to	15.00
1949	"A" Between	.01
1950 to 1952		.01

No shoulder fold

Shoulder Fold

ELIZABETH II, LAUREATED PORTRAIT, 1953 - 1964

Date and Mint Mark	Description	Buying Price
1953	NSF	.01
1953	SF	.50
1954	SF	.01
1955	NSF	50.00
1955	SF	.01
1956 to 1964		.01

Note: You must sort and identify your own coins. Do not expect a dealer to spend hours sorting them for you.

Centennial

ELIZABETH II, TIARA PORTRAIT, 1965 - 1981

Date and Mint Mark	Description	Buying Price
1965 to 1966		.01
1967	Centennial	.01
1968 to 1981		.01

Blunt 5

Pointed 5

ELIZABETH II, TIARA PORTRAIT, 1982 - 1989

Date and Mint Mark	Description	Buying Price
1982 to 1984		.01
1985	Blunt 5	.01
1985	Pointed 5	1.00
1986 to 1989		.01

1867 - 1992

ELIZABETH II, DIADEMED PORTRAIT, 1990 - 1996

Date and Mint Mark	Description	Buying Price
1990 to 1991		.01
1867-1992	Double Date	.01
1993 to 1996		.01

Copper Plated Zinc Coinage

ELIZABETH II, DIADEMED PORTRAIT, 1997 - 2003

Date and Mint Mark	Description	Buying Price
1997 to 2001		.01
1952-2002	Double Date	.01
2003		.01

ELIZABETH II, UNCROWNED PORTRAIT, 2003 - 2006

Date and Mint Mark	Buying Price
2003	.01
2004	.01
2005	.01
2006	.01

Royal Canadian Mint Logo

ELIZABETH II, UNCROWNED PORTRAIT, 2006L - 2007L

Date and Mint Mark	Buying Price
2006L to 2007L	.01

Copper Plated Steel Coinage

Composition Mark

ELIZABETH II, DIADEMED PORTRAIT, 1999P - 2003P

Date and Mint Mark	Description	Buying Price
1999P	Not Issued	5.00
2000P	Not Issued	1,000.00
2001P	Not Issued	.01
1952-2002P	Double Date	.01
2003P		.01

ELIZABETH II, UNCROWNED PORTRAIT, 2003P - 2006P

Date and Mint Mark	Buying Price
2003P	.01
2004P	.01
2005P	.01
2006P	.01

Royal Canadian Mint Logo

ELIZABETH II, UNCROWNED PORTRAIT, 2006L - 2007L

Date and Mint Mark	Buying Price
2006L-2007L	.01

Note: **1.** The 2000P one cent was issued to vending companies for test purposes.
2. Copper plated steel cents are magnetic.

FIVE CENTS SILVER

Plain 4

Crosslet 4

1875H Small date
Short top on 5

1875H Large date
Long top on 5

1900 Small Date

1900 Large Date

VICTORIA 1870 - 1901

Date and Mint Mark	Description	Buying Price
1870		12.00
1871		12.00
1872H		10.00
1874H	Plain 4	17.00
1874H	Crosslet 4	15.00
1875H	Small Date	100.00
1875H	Large Date	200.00
1880H		12.00
1881H		7.00
1882H		10.00
1883H		17.00
1884		75.00
1885		12.00
1886		7.50
1887		15.00
1888		5.00
1889		15.00
1890H		6.00
1891		5.00
1892		6.00
1893		5.00
1894		15.00
1896		4.00
1897		5.00
1898		10.00
1899		4.00
1900	Large Date	15.00
1900	Small Date	4.00
1901		4.00

Note: Buying prices are for coins in **Very Good (VG)** condition.

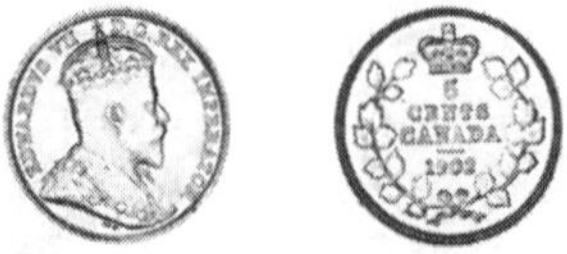

Small H

Large H

Small 8

Large 8

Maple

Holly

EDWARD VII 1902 - 1910

Date and Mint Mark	Description	Buying Price
1902	Plain	1.25
1902	Large H	1.00
1902	Small H	3.00
1903H	Large H	9.00
1903H	Small H	1.25
1903		2.00
1904		1.00
1905		1.00
1906		1.00
1907		1.00
1908	Small 8	3.00
1908	Large 8	10.00
1909	Maple Leaves	1.00
1909	Holly Leaves	6.00
1910	Maple Leaves	6.00
1910	Holly Leaves	1.00

GEORGE V 1911 - 1921

Date and Mint Mark	Buying Price
1911	1.00
1912	1.00
1913	1.00
1914	1.00
1915	5.00
1916	1.00
1917	1.00
1918	1.00
1919	1.00
1920	1.00
1921	1,500.00

FIVE CENTS NICKEL

Near 6

Far 6

GEORGE V 1922 - 1936

Date and Mint Mark	Description	Buying Price
1922 to 1924		.20
1925		45.00
1926	Near 6	1.00
1926	Far 6	85.00
1927 to 1936		.20

Tombac Beaver

Tombac "V"

1947 Maple Leaf

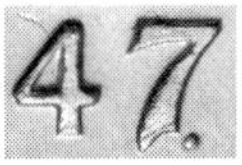

1947 Dot

GEORGE VI 1937 - 1947

Date and Mint Mark	Description	Buying Price
1937	Dot	.10
1938 to 1941		.10
1942	Nickel	.10
1942	Tombac Beaver	.15
1943	Tombac V	.10
1944	Tombav V *	10,000.00
1944 to 1945	Steel V	.10
1946 to 1947		.10
1947	Maple Leaf	.10
1947	Dot	10.00

Geo. VI Obverse

Beaver

1951 High Relief

1951 Comm.

A in GRATIA points to a rim denticle

A in GRATIA points between rim denticles

GEORGE VI 1948 - 1952

Date and Mint Mark	Description	Buying Price
1948	Without "ET IND:IMP"	.10
1949 to 1951		.10
1951	Commemorative	.10
1951	High Relief	200.00
1952		.10

No Shoulder Fold
On the obverse note the flared ends of "I" and the closed top of the "E"

Shoulder Fold
On the obverse note the straight-sided "I" and the open top the the "E"

Note: * This 1944 five cent coin is made of the alloy Tombac. It is brassy in colour when new, and brown when used. It is not the common steel composition of 1944.

Far Maple Leaf

Near Maple Leaf

ELIZABETH II, LAUREATED PORTRAIT, 1953 - 1962

Date and Mint Mark	Description	Buying Price
1953	NSF, far	.10
1953	NSF, near	150.00
1953	SF, near	.10
1953	SF. far	75.00
1954	NSF	3,000.00
1954SF to 1962		.10

1964 Extra Water Line

ELIZABETH II, LAUREATED PORTRAIT, 1963 - 1964

Date and Mint Mark	Description	Buying Price
1963 to 1964		.10
1964	Extra Water Line	5.00

1965 Small Beads Attached Jewel

1965 Large Beads Detached Jewel

ELIZABETH II, TIARA PORTRAIT, 1965 - 1966

Date and Mint Mark	Description	Buying Price
1965	Small Beads	.10
1965	Large Beads	25.00
1966		.10

ELIZABETH II, TIARA PORTRAIT, 1967 - 1989

Date and Mint Mark	Description	Buying Price
1967	Centennial	.10
1968 to 1989		.10

Cupro Nickel Coinage

1867-1992

5¢ 1996 Far 6
"6" Far from"D"
in Canada

5¢ 1996 Near 6
"6" Near "D"
in Canada

ELIZABETH II, DIADEMED PORTRAIT, 1990 - 2001

Date and Mint Mark	Description	Buying Price
1990		.07
1991		.07
1867-1992	Double Date	.07
1993-1995		.07
1996	Far 6	.07
1996	Near 6	.07
1997-2001		.07

Nickel Plated Steel Coinage

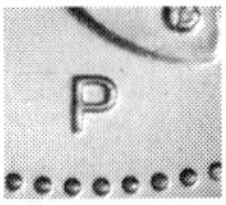

Composition Mark

Double dates 1952 2002P

ELIZABETH II, DIADEMED PORTRAIT, 2000P - 2003P

Date and Mint Mark	Description	Buying Price
1999P	Issued For Testing	5.00
2000P		.10
2001P		.05
1952-2002P	Double Date	.05
2003P		.05

Victory 1945-2005

ELIZABETH II, UNCROWNED PORTRAIT, 2003P - 2006P

Date and Mint Mark	Description	Buying Price
2003-2005P	Beaver	.05
2005P	Victory, 1945-2005	.05
2006P	Beaver	.05

Cupro Nickel Coinage

ELIZABETH II, UNCROWNED PORTRAIT, 2006

Date and Mint Mark	Description	Buying Price
2006		.05

Nickel Plated Steel Coinage

Royal Canadian Mint Logo

ELIZABETH II, UNCROWNED PORTRAIT, 2006L - 2007L

Date and Mint Mark	Description	Buying Price
2006L-2007L	Beaver	.05

Note: The nickel plated steel coins are magnetic.

TEN CENTS

1870 Narrow "0"
Sides of equal thickness

1870 Wide "0"
Right side is thicker

1886 Small 6

1886 Large,
Pointed 6

1886 Large,
Knobbed 6

1892
2 over 1
Large 9

1892
Normal Date
Small 9

1893
Flat-top 3
Medium 9

1893
Round-top 3
Large 9

1899
Small 9s

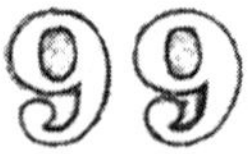

1899
Large 9s

VICTORIA 1870 -1901

Date and Mint Mark	Description	Buying Price
1870	Narrow 0	15.00
1870	Wide 0	20.00
1871		20.00
1871H		20.00
1872H		110.00
1874H		12.00
1875H		235.00
1880H		12.00
1881H		15.00
1882H		15.00
1883H		50.00
1884		185.00
1885		35.00
1886	Small 6	35.00
1886	Large pointed 6	100.00
1886	Large knobbed 6	25.00
1887		50.00
1888		10.00
1889		500.00
1890H		15.00
1891		15.00
1892	Large 9	150.00
1892	Small 9	15.00
1893	Flat Top 3	35.00
1893	Round Top 3	450.00
1894		25.00
1896		10.00
1898		10.00
1899	Small 9	6.00
1899	Large 9	15.00
1900		7.50
1901		7.50

EDWARD VII 1902 - 1910

Date and Mint Mark	Description	Buying Price
1902		3.50
1902H		2.00
1903		7.00
1903H		3.50
1904		5.00
1905		4.00
1906		3.50
1907		1.50
1908		5.00
1909	Victorian Leaves	3.50
1909	Broad Leaves	5.00
1910		3.00

Note: Buying prices are for coins in **Very Good (VG)** condition. Coins of lower grades will command lower prices.

Small Leaves

Broad leaves

GEORGE V 1911 - 1936

Date and Mint Mark	Description	Buying Price
1911		2.75
1912		1.00
1913	Small Leaves	1.00
1913	Broad Leaves	40.00
1914 to 1936		.55

GEORGE VI 1937 - 1947

Date and Mint Mark	Description	Buying Price
1937 to 1947		.55
1947	Maple Leaf	.55

GEORGE VI 1948 - 1952

Date and Mint Mark	Description	Buying Price
1948	Without "ET IND"IMP"	.55
1949 to 1952		.55

ELIZABETH II, LAUREATED PORTRAIT, 1953 - 1964

Date and Mint Mark	Buying Price
1953 to 1964	.55

1969 Small Date

1969 Large Date

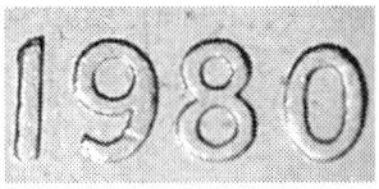

1980 Wide 0

1980 Narrow 0

ELIZABETH II, TIARA PORTRAIT, 1965 - 1989

Date and Mint Mark	Description	Buying Price
1965 to 1966		.55
1967	Centennial	.35
1968	.500 Fine Silver	.27
1968	Nickel	.10
1969	Large Date	7,000.00
1969	Small Date	.10
1970 to 1979		.10
1980	Wide 0	3.00
1980	Narrow 0	.10
1981 to 1989		.10

1867-1992

ELIZABETH II, DIADEMED PORTRAIT, 1990 - 2000

Date and Mint Mark	Description	Buying Price
1990 to 1991		.10
1992	Double Date	.10
1993 to 2000		.10

Nickel Plated Steel Coinage

Composition Mark

Year of the Volunteer

Double dates 1952 2002P

ELIZABETH II, DIADEMED PORTRAIT 1999P - 2003P

Date and Mint Mark	Description	Buying Price
1999P		5.00
2000P		300.00
2001P	Volunteers	.10
2001P	Bluenose	.10
1952-2002P	Double Date	.10
2003P		.10

ELIZABETH II, UNCROWNED PORTRAIT, 2003P - 2006P

Date and Mint Mark	Buying Price
2003P	.10
2004P	.10
2005P	.10
2006P	.10

Royal Canadian Mint Logo

ELIZABETH II, UNCROWNED PORTRAIT, 2006L - 2007L

Date and Mint Mark	Buying Price
2006L	.10
2007L	.10

TWENTY-FIVE CENTS

Narrow 0

Wide 0

6 over 3

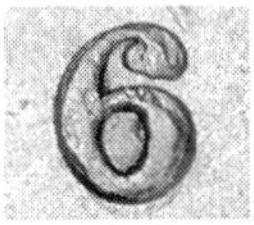

6 over 6

VICTORIA 1870 - 1901

Date and Mint Mark	Description	Buying Price
1870		17.50
1871		20.00
1871H		20.00
1872H		10.00
1874H		7.50
1875H		275.00
1880H	Narrow O	50.00
1880H	Wide O	100.00
1881H		20.00
1882H		22.00
1883H		15.00
1885		125.00
1886		110.00
1886	6 over 3	60.00
1886	6 over 6	75.00
1887		100.00
1888		20.00
1889		125.00
1890H		20.00
1891		75.00
1892		17.50
1893		100.00
1894		22.50
1899		10.00
1900		10.00
1901		7.50

Small crown

Large crown

EDWARD VII 1902 - 1910

Date and Mint Mark	Description	Buying Price
1902		7.00
1902H		5.00
1903		7.00
1904		10.00
1905		7.00
1906	Small Crown	1,000.00
1906	Large Crown	5.00
1907		4.00
1908		7.00
1909		5.00
1910		5.00

GEORGE V 1911 - 1936

Date and Mint Mark	Description	Buying Price
1911		5.00
1912 to 1914		1.70
1915		10.00
1916 to 1920		1.70
1921		5.00
1927		15.00
1928 to 1936		1.70
1936	Dot	15.00

Note: Buying prices are for coins in **Very Good (VG)** condition. Coins with excessive wear, holed or bent will be discount from the listed price.

1947 Dot

1947 Maple Leaf

GEORGE VI 1937 - 1947

Date and Mint Mark	Description	Buying Price
1937 to 1947		1.35
1947	Maple Leaf	1.35
1947	Dot	30.00

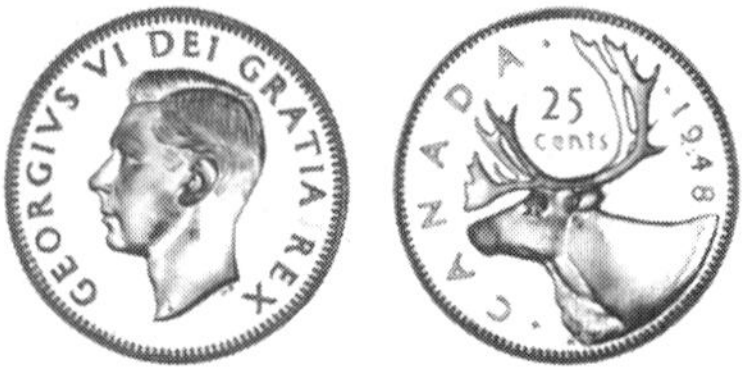

GEORGE VI 1948 - 1952

Date and Mint Mark	Descripton	Buying Price
1948	Without "ET IND:IMP"	1.35
1949 to 1952		1.35

ELIZABETH II, LAUREATED PORTRAIT, 1953 - 1964

Date and Mint Mark	Description	Buying Price
1953	Large Date	1.35
1953	Small Date	1.35
1954 to 1964		1.35

Centennial

RCMP

1973 Small Bust
120 Obverse Beads
Far from Rim

1973 Large Bust
132 Obverse Beads
Near Rim

ELIZABETH II, TIARA PORTRAIT, 1965 - 1973

Date and Mint Mark	Description	Buying Price
1965 to 1966		1.35
1967	Centennial	.85
1968	.500 Fine Silver	.65
1968 to 1972	Nickel	.25
1973	Small Bust	.25
1973	Large Bust	65.00

ELIZABETH II, TIARA PORTRAIT, 1974 - 1989

Date and Mint Mark	Buying Price
1974 to 1989	.25

Note: Victoria, Edward and George V quarters must be Very **Good (VG)** or better.

ELIZABETH II, DIADEMED PORTRAIT, 1990 - 1991

Date and Mint Mark	Buying Price
1990	.25
1991	1.00

CANADA 125 ANNIVERSARY

Common Obverse

New Brunswick

Northwest Territories

Newfoundland

Manitoba

Yukon

Alberta

Prince Edward Island

Ontario

Nova Scotia

Quebec

Saskatchewan

British Columbia

ELIZABETH II, DIADEMED PORTRAIT, 1992

Date and Mint Mark	Description	Buying Price
1992	New Brunswick, Medal	.25
1992	New Brunswick, Coinage	15.00
1992	Northwest Territories	.25
1992	Newfoundland	.25
1992	Manitoba	.25
1992	Yukon	.25
1992	Alberta	.25
1992	Prince Edward Island	.25
1992	Ontario	.25
1992	Nova Scotia	.25
1992	Quebec	.25
1992	Saskatchewan	.25
1992	British Columbia	.25

ELIZABETH II, DIADEMED PORTRAIT, 1993 - 2001

Date and Mint Mark	Description	Buying Price
1993 to 1996		.25
2001		.25

1999 MILLENNIUM QUARTERS

Common Obverse

January

February

March

April

May

June

July

August

September

October

November

December

ELIZABETH II, DIADEMED PORTRAIT, 1999

Date and Mint Mark	Description	Buying Price
1999	January	.25
1999	February	.25
1999	March	.25
1999	April	.25
1999	May	.25
1999	June	.25
1999	July	.25
1999	August	.25
1999	September	.25
1999	October	.25
1999	November	.25
1999	December	.25

2000 MILLENNIUM QUARTERS

Common Obverse

January

February

March

April

May

June

July

August

September

October

November

December

ELIZABETH II, DIADEMED PORTRAIT, 2000

Date and Mint Mark	Description	Buying Price
2000	January, Pride	.25
2000	February, Ingenuity	.25
2000	March, Achievement	.25
2000	April, Health	.25
2000	May, Natural Legacy	.25
2000	June, Harmony	.25
2000	July, Celebration	.25
2000	August, Family	.25
2000	September, Wisdom	.25
2000	October. Creativity	.25
2000	November, Freedom	.25
2000	December, Community	.25

Note: If a date is not listed then it was not issed for circulation.

Nickel Plated Steel Coinage

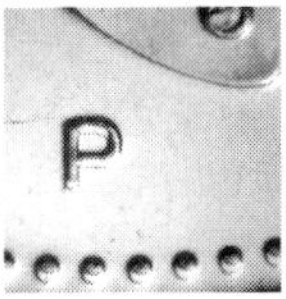

Composition Mark

ELIZABETH II, DIADEMED PORTRAIT, 1999P - 2001P

Date and Mint Mark	Buying Price
1999P	5.00
2000P	2,500.00
2001P	.25

ELIZABETH II, DIADEMED PORTRAIT, 2002P - 2003P

Date and Mint Mark	Description	Buying Price
1952-2002P	Canada Day, Double Date	.25
1952-2002P	Caribou, Double Date	.25
2003P		.25

First Settlement 2004

Poppy 2004

Alberta
2005

Saskatchewan
2005

Year of the Veteran
2006

Breast Cancer
2006

ELIZABETH II, UNCROWNED PORTRAIT, 2003P - 2006P

Date and Mint Mark	Description	Buying Price
2003P	Caribou	.25
2004P	Caribou	.25
2004P	First Settlement	.25
2004P	Poppy	.25
2005P	Caribou	.25
2005P	Alberta	.25
2005P	Saskatchewan	.25
2005P	Year of the Veteran	.25
2006P	Caribou	.25
2006P	Breast Cancer	.25

Medal of Bravery

Royal
Canadian
Mint Logo

ELIZABETH II, UNCROWNED PORTRAIT, 2006L - 2007L

Date and Mint Mark	Description	Buying Price
2006L	Caribou	.25
2006L	Medal of Bravery	.25
2007L	Caribou	.25

VANCOUVER WINTER OLYMPIC AND PARALYMPIC GAMES

Common Obv.

Curling

Ice Hockey

Biathlon

Alpine Skiing

Paralympic Obv.

Wheelchair Curling

ELIZABETH II, UNCROWNED PORTRAIT, 2007

Date and Mint Mark	Description	Buying Price
2007	Curling	.25
2007	Ice Hockey	.25
2007	Biathlon	.25
2007	Alpine Skiing	.25
2007	Wheelchair Curling	.25

FIFTY CENTS

L.C.W.

No L.C.W.

VICTORIA 1870 - 1901

Date and Mint Mark	Description	Buying Price
1870	Without L.C.W.	600.00
1870	With L.C.W.	35.00
1871		40.00
1871H		90.00
1872H		40.00
1881H		40.00
1888		225.00
1890H		750.00
1892		60.00
1894		250.00
1898		50.00
1899		110.00
1900		35.00
1901		35.00

EDWARD VII 1902 - 1910

Date and Mint Mark	Description	Buying Price
1902		10.00
1903H		10.00
1904		65.00
1905		65.00
1906		6.50
1907		4.00
1908		10.00
1909		6.50
1910	Victorian Leaves	10.00
1910	Edwardian Leaves	5.25

GEORGE V 1911 - 1936

Date and Mint Mark	Description	Buying Price
1911		9.00
1912		6.50
1913		6.50
1914		6.50
1916		4.00
1917		4.00
1918		4.00
1919		4.00
1920	Wide 0	9.00
1920	Narrow 0	4.00
1921		15,000.00
1929		6.00
1931		10.00
1932		85.00
1934		10.00
1936		15.00

Straight "7"
No Maple Leaf

Curved "7"
No Maple Leaf

Straight "7"
With Maple Leaf

Curved "7"
With Maple Leaf

Note: Coins must grade **Very Good** or better. Badly worn coins (good) will be priced lower.

GEORGE VI 1937 - 1947

Date and Mint Mark	Description	Buying Price
1937 to 1946		2.75
1947	Straight "7"	2.75
1947	Curved "7"	2.75
1947	M.L., Straight "7"	10.00
1947	M.L., Curved "7"	800.00

GEORGE VI 1948 - 1952

Date and Mint Mark	Description	Buying Price
1948	Without "ET IND:IMP"	60.00
1949 to 1952		2.75

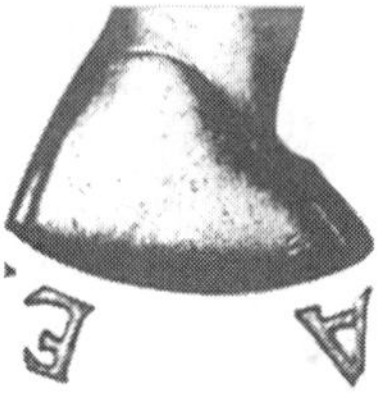
No shoulder fold

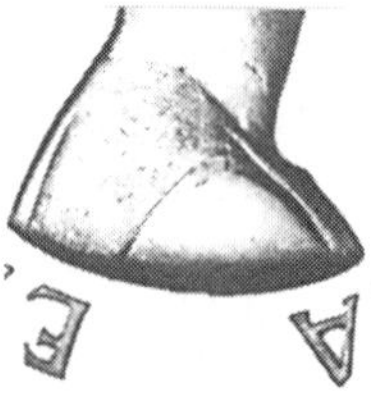
Shoulder fold

Small date

Large date

ELIZABETH II, LAUREATED PORTRAIT, 1953 - 1964

Date and Mint Mark	Description	Buying Price
1953	NSF, SD	2.75
1953	NSF, LD	3.00
1953	SF, LD	2.75
1954 to 1964		2.75

ELIZABETH II, TIARA PORTRAIT, 1965 - 1967

Date and Mint Mark	Description	Buying Price
1965 to 1966		2.75
1967	Centennial	2.75

1978 Square Jewels

1978 Round Jewels

1982 - 118 Large Beads

1982 - 120 Small beads

ELIZABETH II, TIARA PORTRAIT, 1968 - 1989

Date and Mint Mark	Description	Buying Price
1968 to 1977		.50
1978	Square Jewels	.50
1978	Round Jewels	1.00
1979 to 1981		.50
1982	Large Beads	.50
1982	Small Beads	15.00
1983 to 1989		.50

ELIZABETH II, DIADEMED PORTRAIT, 1990 - 2000

Date and Mint Mark	Description	Buying Price
1990 to 1991		.50
1867-1992	Double Date	.50
1993 to 1996		.50
1997 to 2000	Modified Reverse	.50

Note: Fifty cents 2002P to 2007L are issued only in rolls of 25, by the Mint.

Nickel Plated Steel Coinage

Composition Mark

ELIZABETH II, DIADEMED PORTRAIT, 1999P - 2001P

Date and Mint Mark	Buying Price
1999P	5.00
2000P	2,500.00
2001P	.50
2002P-2004P	.50

ELIZABETH II, IMPERIAL STATE CROWN PORTRAIT, 2002P

Date and Mint Mark	Description	Buying Price
1952-2002P	Jubilee Portrait	.50

ELIZABETH II, UNCROWNED PORTRAIT, 2005P - 2006P, and 2006L-2007L

Date and Mint Mark	Buying Price
2003P-2006P	.50
2006L-2007L	.50

SILVER DOLLARS

1935 Obverse

1936 Obverse

1937 to 1947 Obverse

1935 Reverse

1939 Parliament

1949 Newfoundland

Blunt 7

Pointed 7

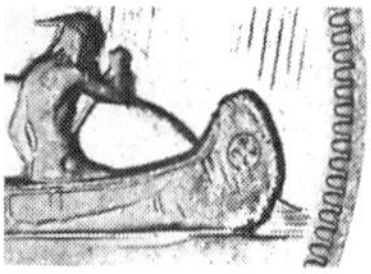
1952 Water Lines

1952 No Water Lines

1947 Maple Leaf

1947 Dot

GEORGE V 1935 - 1936

Date and Mint Mark	Description	Buying VF Price
1935	Silver Jubilee	15.00
1936	Voyageur	10.00

GEORGE VI 1937 - 1946

Date and Mint Mark	Description	Buying VF Price
1937	Voyageur	10.00
1938	Voyageur	30.00
1939	Royal Visit	8.00
1945	Voyageur	90.00
1946	Voyageur	20.00

GEORGE VI 1947 - 1952

Date and Mint Mark	Description	Buying VF Price
1947	Blunt 7	55.00
1947	Pointed 7	75.00
1947 Dot	Pointed 7	80.00
1947	Maple Leaf	100.00
1948	Dei Gratia	650.00
1949	Newfoundland	10.00
1950	Voyageur	8.00
1950	Arnprior	8.00
1951	Voyageur	8.00
1951	Arnprior	25.00
1952	Water Lines	8.00
1952	Arnprior	10.00
1952	No Water Lines	8.00

IMPORTANT: The silver dollar buying prices are for problem free coins in **Very Fine (VF)** condition. Damaged coins will bring lower prices.

1953 Obverse

1959 Reverse

1964 Charlottetown

1958 British Columbia

1965 Reverse

1967 Centennial

1955 4 Water Lines

1955 2 ½ Water Lines

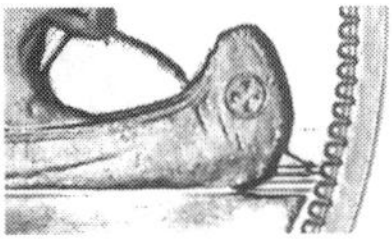

1957 4 Water Lines

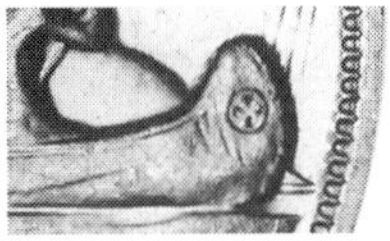

1957 2 ½ Water Lines

ELIZABETH II, LAUREATED PORTRAIT, 1953 - 1964

Date and Mint Mark	Description	Buying VF Price
1953	Voyageur	8.00
1954	Voyageur	8.00
1955	Voyageur	8.00
1955 Arnprior	2 ½ Waterlines	15.00
1956	Voyageur	8.00
1957	Voyageur	8.00
1957 Arnprior	One Waterline	8.00
1958	British Columbia	8.00
1959	Voyageur	8.00
1960	Voyageur	8.00

ELIZABETH II, TIARA PORTRAIT, 1965 - 1967

Date and Mint Mark	Description	Buying VF Price
1961	Voyageur	8.00
1962	Voyageur	8.00
1963	Voyageur	8.00
1964	Charlottetown	8.00
1965	Voyageur, Medal	8.00
1965	Voyageur, Coinage	1,000.00
1966	Voyageur	8.00
1966 Sm Beads	Voyageur	1,000.00
1967	Centennial, Medal	8.00
1967	Centennial, Coinage	1,000.00

DIE AXIS

The obverse design is considered the primary side of the coin. The die axis is the relationship of the reverse design to the obverse. Consider the obverse die, usually the anvil die in a press, stationary and when installed is the point of reference. The reverse die (moving hammer die) may be turned or set at any of 360 degrees in relation to the set obverse die. If the obverse die is identified by an upright arrow (↑) then the reverse die may be represented by a second arrow(↑). These arrows form a relationship. Illustrated below are two common die positions:

Coinage Axis: ↑↓

Obverse die: ↑

Reverse die is set 180 degrees opposite: ↓

Medal Axis: ↑↑

Obverse die:

Reverse die is set in the matching direction: ↑

NICKEL DOLLARS

Common Obverse

Voyageur Reverse

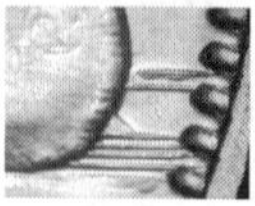

1968 Island

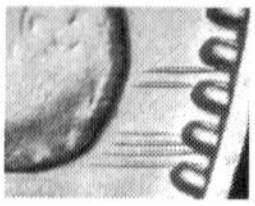

1968 No Island

Manitoba

British Columbia

Prince Edward Island

Winnipeg

Constitution

Jacques Cartier

ELIZABETH II, TIARA PORTRAIT, 1968 - 1973

Date and Mint Mark	Description	Buying Price
1968	Voyageur	1.00
1968	Small Island	5.00
1968	No Island	2.00
1969	Voyageur	1.00
1970	Manitoba	1.00
1971	British Columbia	1.00
1972	Voyageur	1.00
1973	P.E.I.	1.00

ELIZABETH II, TIARA PORTRAIT, 1974 - 1986

Date and Mint Mark	Description	Buying Price
1974	Winnipeg	1.00
1975 to 1981	Voyageur	1.00
1982	Constitution, Medal	1.00
1982	Consitution, Coinage	500.00
1983	Voyageur	1.00
1984	Jacques Cartier	1.00
1985	Voyageur	1.00
1986	Voyageur	1.00

NICKEL BRONZE DOLLARS

ELIZABETH II, TIARA PORTRAIT, 1987 - 1989

Date and Mint Mark	Description	Buying Price
1987	Loon, Unc	1.00
1987	Loon, Proof	4.00
1988	Loon	1.00
1989	Loon	1.00

ELIZABETH II, DIADEMED PORTRAIT, 1992 - 1993

Date and Mint Mark	Description	Buying Price
1867-1992	Double Date	1.00
1993	Loon	1.00

ELIZABETH II, DIADEMED PORTRAIT, 1990 - 1991

Date and Mint Mark	Description	Buying Price
1990 to 1991	Loon	1.00

ELIZABETH II, DIADEMED PORTRAIT, 1994

Date and Mint Mark	Description	Buying Price
1994	Remembrance, Unc	1.00
1994	Remembrance, Proof	4.00
1994	Loon	1.00

CANADA 125 ANNIVERSARY

ELIZABETH II, DIADEMED PORTRAIT, 1992

Date and Mint Mark	Description	Buying Price
1992	Unc	1.00

ELIZABETH II, DIADEMED PORTRAIT, 1995

Date and Mint Mark	Description	Buying Price
1995	Peacekeeping, Unc	1.00
1995	Peacekeeping, Proof	4.00

IMPORTANT: Do not clean your coins. Coins should be handled carefully. Only experts should consider cleaning. If you are not an expert, the results can be disastrous.

Note: Proof issues of 1987, 1992, 1994 and 1995 were issued by the Numismatic Deptartment of the Royal Canadian Mint.

ELIZABETH II, DIADEMED PORTRAIT, 1995 - 1996

Date and Mint Mark	Description	Buying Price
1995	Loon	1.00
1996	Loon	1.00
1997 to 2001	Not Issued	

ELIZABETH II, DIADEMED PORTRAIT, 2002

Date and Mint Mark	Description	Buying Price
1952-2002	Jubilee	2.00

2004 Lucky Loonie

2005 Terry Fox

2006 Lucky Loonie

ELIZABETH II, UNCROWNED PORTRAIT, 2003 - 2006

Date and Mint Mark	Description	Buying Price
2003	Loon	1.00
2004	Loon	1.00
2004	Lucky Loonie	1.00
2005	Loon	1.00
2005	Terry Fox	1.00
2006	Loon	1.00
2006	Lucky Loonie	1.00

Royal Canadian Mint Logo

ELIZABETH II, UNCROWNED PORTRAIT, 2006L - 2007L

Date and Mint Mark	Description	Buying Price
2006L	Loon	1.00
2007L	Loon	1.00

TWO DOLLAR COINS

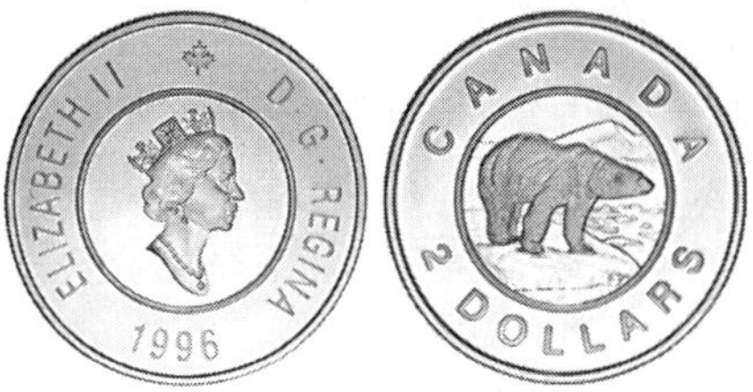

ELIZABETH II, DIADEMED PORTRAIT 1996 - 1998

Date and Mint Mark	Description	Buying Price
1996	Polar Bear	2.00
1997	Polar Bear	2.00
1998	Polar Bear	2.00

ELIZABETH II, DIADEMED PORTRAIT, 2001 - 2003

Date and Mint Mark	Description	Buying Price
2001	Polar Bear	2.00
1952-2002	Double Date	2.00
2003	Polar Bear	2.00

ELIZABETH II, DIADEMED PORTRAIT, 1999

Date and Mint Mark	Description	Buying Price
1999	Nunavut	2.00

ELIZABETH II, UNCROWNED PORTRAIT, 2003 - 2006

Date and Mint Mark	Description	Buying Price
2003	Polar Bear	2.00
2004	Polar Bear	2.00
2005	Polar Bear	2.00
2006	Polar Bear	2.00

ELIZABETH II, DIADEMED PORTRAIT, 2000

Date and Mint Mark	Description	Buying Price
2000	Polar Bears	2.00

1996-2006 10th Anniversary

1996-2006 10th Anniversary "Churchill"

ELIZABETH II, UNCROWNED PORTRAIT, 2006

Date and Mint Mark	Description	Buying Price
2006	10th Anniv.	2.00
2006	Churchill	2.00

Royal Canadian Mint Logo

ELIZABETH II, UNCROWNED PORTRAIT, 2006 - 2007

Date and Mint Mark	Description	Buying Price
2006L	Polar Bear	2.00
2007L	Polar Bear	2.00

CIRCULATING GOLD COINS

SOVEREIGNS

EDWARD VII 1908 - 1910

Date and Mint Mark	Buying VF Price
1908C	1,200.00
1909C	165.00
1910C	165.00

GEORGE V 1911 - 1919

Date and Mint Mark	Buying VF Price
1911C	165.00
1913C	300.00
1914C	200.00
1916C	10,000.00
1917C	165.00
1918C	165.00
1919C	165.00

FIVE DOLLARS

GEORGE V 1912 - 1914

Date and Mint Mark	Buying VF Price
1912	175.00
1913	175.00
1914	200.00

TEN DOLLARS

GEORGE V 1912 - 1914

Date and Mint Mark	Buying VF Price
1912	350.00
1913	350.00
1914	375.00

IMPORTANT: Do not clean your coins. Coins should be handled carefully. Only experts should consider cleaning. If you are not an expert, the results can be disastrous.

COLLECTORS ISSUES

The numismatic department of the Royal Canadian Mint issued specially struck and packaged coins starting in 1954. The coins were issued for collectors and as a result are of high quality. The dealer buying prices listed below are for single coins and sets in their original packaging and condition. Coins or sets which have been mishandled or damaged are discounted from the prices listed. Beginning in 1971 the numismatic department of the Royal Canadian Mint issued silver dollars for collectors in two conditions, proof and uncirculated. Proof condition dollars were issued in black leatherette boxes while uncirculated dollars were issued in a clear plastic container.

ONE CENT

Date	Description	Buying Price
2003	Selectively gold plated	25.00

SILVER THREE CENTS

Date	Description	Buying Price
2001	3 Cent Beaver	10.00

SILVER FIVE CENTS

2000-2002
Common Obv.

Les Voltigeurs
de Québec

Royal Military
College of Canada

85th Anniv. Battle
for Vimy Ridge

Date	Description	Buying Price
2000	Les Voltigeurs de Québec	5.00
2001	Royal Military College, Canada	5.00
2002	85th Anniversary, Vimy Ridge	10.00

60th Anniversary D-Day 1944-2004

60th Anniversary VE-Day 1945-2005

1945-2005
Selectively
gold platead

Date	Description	Buying Price
2004	60th Anniv. D-Day	30.00
2005	60th Anniv. VE-Day	15.00
2006	1945-2005 Gold plated	15.00

SILVER TEN CENTS

Caboto

Date	Description	Buying Price
1997	Caboto	10.00

100th Anniv. Credit Unions in N.A. 2000

Year of the Volunteers, 2001

Canadian Open Golf, 2004

Date	Description	Buying Price
2000	100th Anniv. Credit Unions	5.00
2001	Int'l Year of Volunteers	5.00
2004	Canadian Open Golf	5.00

TWENTY-FIVE CENTS
125TH ANNIVERSARY 1867-1992

For the complete 12-coin set of the 1867-1992, 125th Anniversary see pages 24 and 25. The set was minted in both nickel and silver

January - New Brunswick

Date	Description	No. of Coins	Buying Price
1992	125th Anniversary silver proof set	13	80.00
1992	Single silver coin	1	5.00
1992	125 Anniversary nickel souvenier set	13	6.00

TWENTY-FIVE CENTS
1999 MILLENNIUM SET

For the complete 24-coin set of the 1999-2000 millennium celebration see pages 25 and 26. The coins were issued in both nickel and silver.

January 1999

1999 Millennium Medallion

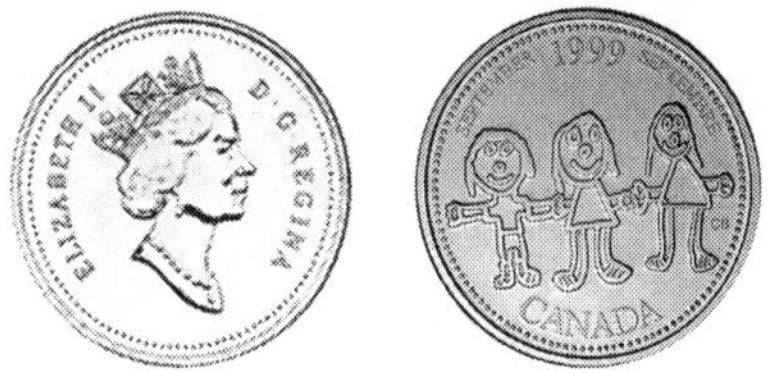

September 1999 Mule
Obverse has no denomination

November 1999 Mule
Obverse has no denomination

Date	Description	No. of Coins	Buying Price
1999	12 coin set and 1999 medallion		6.00
1999	September, no denomination		1,000.00
1999	November, no denomination		100.00
1999	Medallion		2.00
1999	12 coin silver set		80.00
1999	Single silver coin		5.00

TWENTY-FIVE CENTS

2000 MILLENNIUM

January 2000, for complete set see page 26.

2000 Millennium Medallion

2000 Mule
Coin Obverse with Medallion Obverse

Date	Description	Buying Price
2000	12-coin, medallion	8.00
2000	Medallion	2.00
2000	Coin; medallion mule	300.00
2000	12-coin silver set	80.00
2000	Single silver coin	5.00

CANADA'S FIRST COLOURIZED COIN

Obv. 2000-2003

Date	Description	Buying Price
2000	January	20.00

CANADA DAY SERIES

Canada Day 2000

Canada Day 2001

Canada Day 2002

Canada Day 2003

Obv. 2004-2006

Canada Day, 2004

Moose 2004

Canada Day 2005

Canada Day 2006

Canada Day 2007

CANADA DAY SERIES (cont.)

Date	Description	Buying Price
2000	Canada Day 2000	50.00
2001P	Canada Day 2001	7.50
2002P	Canada Day 2002	7.50
2003P	Canada Day 2003	10.00
2004P	Canada Day 2004	15.00
2004P	Moose 2004	15.00
2005P	Canada Day 2005	10.00
2006P	Canada Day 2006	10.00
2007L	Canada Day 2007	10.00

CHRISTMAS DAY

2004 Santa Claus

2005
Christmas Stocking

2006 Santa in Sleigh

Date	Description	Buying Price
2004	Santa Claus	15.00
2005	Christmas Stocking	12.50
2006	Santa in Sleigh	7.50

2004 Poppy

2005 Poppy

2006 Liberation

Date	Description	Buying Price
2004	Poppy, Silver	10.00
2005P	Poppy	5.00
2006P	Liberation, Silver	35.00

QUEBEC WINTER CARNIVAL

Date	Description	Buying Price
2006P	Quebec Winter Carnival	15.00

BREAST CANCER AWARENESS

This coin was encased in a plastic bookmark.

Date	Description	Buying Price
2006P	Breast Cancer Awareness	5.00

HOCKEY SERIES (Gift and Holiday Sets)

2005-2006 HOCKEY SEASON

Common Obv.

Montreal Canadiens

Ottawa Senators

Toronto Maple Leafs

2006-2007 HOCKEY SEASON

Common Obv.

Calgary Flames

Edmonton Oilers

Montreal Canadiens

Ottawa Senators

Toronto Maple Leafs

Vancouver Canucks

Date	Description	Buying Price
2006P	Montreal Canadiens	8.00
2006P	Ottawa Senators	8.00
2006P	Toronto Maple Leafs	8.00
2007L	Calgary Flames	8.00
2007L	Edmonton Oilers	8.00
2007L	Montreal Canadiens	8.00
2007L	Ottawa Senators	8.00
2007L	Toronto Maple Leafs	8.00
2007L	Vancouver Canucks	8.00

80TH BIRTHDAY QUEEN ELIZABETH II

Date	Description	Buying Price
2006	80th Birthday Queen Elizabeth II	8.00

BIRD SERIES

Date	Description	Buying Price
2007	Hummingbird	10.00

PROOF SILVER FIFTY CENTS
WILD LIFE SERIES

Atlantic Puffin

Whooping Crane

Gray Jays

White Tailed Ptarmigans

Date	Description	Buying Price
1995	Atlantic Puffins	6.00
1995	Whooping Crane	6.00

Date	Description	Buying Price
1995	Gray Jays	6.00
1995	White Tailed Ptarmigans	6.00

Moose Calf

Wood Ducklings

Cougar Kittens

Black Bear Cubs

Date	Description	Buying Price
1996	Moose Calf	10.00
1996	Wood Ducklings	10.00

Date	Description	Buying Price
1996	Cougar Kittens	10.00
1996	Black Bear Cubs	10.00

Newfoundland

Nova Scotia Duck Tolling Retriever

Labrador Retriever

Canadian Eskimo Dog

Date	Description	Buying Price
1997	Newfoundland	7.00
1997	Nova Scotia Duck Tolling Retriever	7.00

Date	Description	Buying Price
1997	Labrador Retriever	7.00
1997	Canadian Eskimo Dog	7.00

PROOF SILVER FIFTY CENTS
WILD LIFE SERIES

Killer Whale

Humpback Whale

Beluga Whale

Blue Whale

Date	Description	Buying Price
1998	Killer Whale	7.00
1998	Humpback Whale	7.00

Date	Description	Buying Price
1998	Beluga Whale	7.00
1998	Blue Whale	7.00

Tonkinese

Lynx

Cymric

Cougar

Date	Description	Buying Price
1999	Tonkinese	12.00
1999	Lynx	12.00

Date	Description	Buying Price
1999	Cymric	12.00
1999	Cougar	12.00

Bald Eagle

Osprey

Great Horned Owl

Red-Tailed Hawk

Date	Description	Buying Price
2000	Bald Eagle	7.00
2000	Osprey	7.00

Date	Description	Buying Price
2000	Great Horned Owl	7.00
2000	Red-Tailed Hawk	7.00

PROOF SILVER FIFTY CENTS
SPORTS SERIES

Skating

Skiing

Soccer

Auto Racing

Date	Description	Buying Price
1998	Skating	6.00
1998	Skiing	6.00

Date	Description	Buying Price
1998	Soccer	6.00
1998	Auto Racing	6.00

Golf

Yacht Race

Football

Basketball

Date	Description	Buying Price
1999	Golf	8.00
1999	Yacht Race	6.00

Date	Description	Buying Price
1999	Football	6.00
1999	Basketball	6.00

Hockey

Curling

Steeplechase

Bowling

Date	Description	Buying Price
2000	Hockey	7.00
2000	Curling	6.00

Date	Description	Buying Price
2000	Steeplechase	6.00
2000	Bowling	6.00

PROOF SILVER FIFTY CENTS
CANADIAN FESTIVALS SERIES

Quebec Winter Carnival (Quebec)

Toonik Tyme (Nunavut)

Newfoundland and Labrador Folk Festival (Newfoundland)

Festival of Fathers (Prince Edward Island)

Annapolis Valley Blossom Festival (Nova Scotia)

Stratford Festival of Canada (Ontario)

Folklorama (Manitoba)

Calgary Stampede (Alberta)

Squamish Days Logger Sports (British Columbia)

Yukon Festival (Yukon)

Back to Batoche (Saskatchewan)

Great Northern Arts Festival (Northwest Territories)

Festival Acadien de Caraquet (New Brunswick)

Date	Description	Price
2001	Québec	5.00
2001	Nunavut	5.00
2001	Newfoundland	5.00
2001	Prince Edward Island	5.00
2002	Nova Scotia	5.00
2002	Ontario	5.00
2002	Manitoba	5.00
2002	Alberta	5.00
2002	British Columbia	5.00
2003	Yukon	5.00
2003	Saskatchewan	5.00
2003	Northwest Territories	5.00
2003	New Brunswick	5.00
2001-03	Set Can. Festivals (13 coins)	75.00

PROOF SILVER FIFTY CENTS
CANADIAN FOLKLORE AND LEGENDS SERIES

The Sled

The Maiden's Cave

Les Petits Sauteux

The Pig That Wouldn't

Shoemaker in Heaven

Le Vaisseau Fantome

Date	Description	Price
2001	The Sled	5.00
2001	The Maiden's Cave	5.00
2001	Les Petits Sauteux	5.00

Date	Description	Price
2002	The Pig That Wouldn't	5.00
2002	Shoemaker in Heaven	5.00
2002	Le Vaisseau Fantome	5.00

FLOWER SERIES

Golden Tulip

Golden Daffodil

Golden Lily

Golden Rose

Golden Daisy

Golden Forget Me Not

Date	Description	Price
2002	Golden Tulip	35.00
2003	Golden Daffodil	17.50
2004	Golden Lily	17.50

Date	Description	Price
2005	Golden Rose	17.50
2006	Golden Daisy	20.00
2007	Golden Forget Me Not	17.50

PROOF SILVER FIFTY CENTS
COAT OF ARMS OF CANADA

Kruger-Gray 1953

Shingles 1954-1958

Shingles 1959-1996

Bursey-Sabourin
1997-2005

Date	Description	Buying Price
2004	Kruger-Gray, 1953	10.00
2004	Shingles, 1954-1958	10.00
2004	Shingles 1959-1996	10.00
2004	Bursey-Sabourin, 1997-2005	10.00

CANADIAN BUTTERFLY COLLECTION

Canadian Tiger Swallowtail

Canadian Clouded Sulpher

Monarch

Spangled Fritillary

Short-tailed Swallowtail

Silvery Blue

Date	Description	Buying Price
2003	Canadian Tiger Swallowtail	18.00
2004	Canadian Clouded Sulpher	18.00
2005	Monarch	25.00
2005	Spangled Fritillary	25.00
2006	Short-tailed Swallowtail	30.00
2007	Silvery Blue	18.00

QUEST FOR PEACE AND FREEDOM DURING SECOND WORLD WAR

Battle of Britain

Liberation of Netherlands

Conquest of Sicily

Battle of the Scheldt

Raid on Dieppe

Battle of the Atlantic

Date	Description	Buying Price
2005	Battle of Britain	12.50
2005	Liberation of Netherlands	12.50
2005	Conquest of Sicily	12.50
2005	Battle of the Scheldt	12.50
2005	Raid on Dieppe	12.50
2005	Battle of the Atlantic	12.50

HOCKEY LEGENDS

Jean Beliveau

Guy Lafleur

Jacques Plante

Maurice Richard

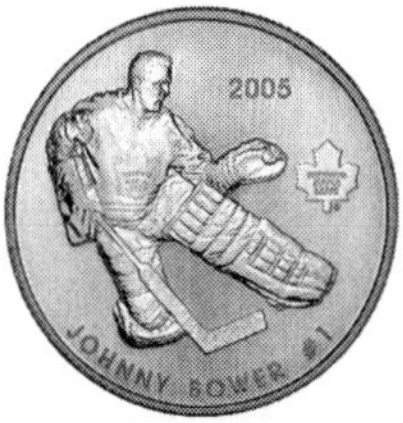

Johnny Bower

Tim Horton

Darryl Sittler

Dave Keon

Date	Description	Buying Price
2005	Jean Beliveau	12.50
2005	Guy Lafleur	12.50
2005	Jacques Plante	12.50
2005	Maurice Richard	12.50
2005	Johnny Bower	12.50
2005	Tim Horton	12.50
2005	Darryl Sittler	12.50
2005	Dave Keon	12.50

SILVER PROOF-LIKE DOLLARS

Single dollars, in either cellophane or pliofilm packaging, were issued by the Royal Canadian Mint for collectors. Illustrations of these dollars can be found on page 32.

Date	Description	Buying Price
1954	Voyageur	175.00
1955	Voyageur	110.00
1955	Arnprior	225.00
1956	Voyageur	70.00
1957	Voyageur	45.00
1958	British Columbia	30.00
1959	Voyageur	11.00
1960	Voyageur	11.00
1961	Voyageur	9.00
1962	Voyageur	9.00
1963	Voyageur	9.00
1964	Charlottetown	9.00

CASED NICKEL DOLLARS

1970 Manitoba

1971 British Columbia

1973 Prince Edward Island

1974 Winnipeg

1982 Constitution

1984 Jacques Cartier

Date	Description	Buying Price
1970	Manitoba	1.50
1971	British Columbia	1.50
1972	Voyageur	1.50
1973	Prince Edward Island	1.50
1974	Winnipeg	1.50
1975	Voyageur	1.50
1976	Voyageur	1.50
1982	Constitution	2.00
1984	Jacques Cartier	2.00

Note: Coins must be as issued in clam style Mint cases.

CASED SILVER DOLLARS

Common Obverse

1971 British Columbia

1973 R.C.M.P.

1974 Winnipeg Centennial

1975 Calgary

1976 Library of Parliament

1977 Silver Jubilee

1978 Commonwealth Games

1979 Griffon Tricentennial

Date	Description	Buying Price
1971	British Columbia Centennial	4.50
1972	Voyageur	4.50
1973	R.C.M.P.	4.50
1974	Winnipeg Centennial	4.50
1975	Calgary Stampede	4.50

Date	Description	Buying Price
1976	Library of Parliament	4.50
1977	Silver Jubilee	4.50
1978	Commonwealth Games	4.50
1979	Griffon Tricentennial	4.50

CASED SILVER DOLLARS

1980 Arctic Territories

1981 Trans-Canada Railway

1982 Regina Centennial

1983 World University Games

1984 Toronto Sesquicentennial

1985 National Parks Centannial

1986 Vancouver Centennial

1987 John Davis Strait

1988 Saint-Maurice Ironworks

Date	Description	Buying Price
1980	Arctic Territories Centennial	4.50
1981	Trans-Canada Railway (PR)	4.50
1981	Trans-Canada Railway (UNC)	4.50
1982	Regina Centennial (PR)	4.50
1982	Regina Centennial (UNC)	4.50
1983	World University Games (PR)	4.50
1983	World University Games (UNC)	4.50
1984	Toronto Sesquicentennial (PR)	4.50
1984	Toronto Sesquicentennial (UNC)	4.50

Date	Description	Buying Price
1985	National Parks Centennial (PR)	6.00
1985	National Parks Centennial (UNC)	4.50
1986	Vancouver Centennial (PR)	6.00
1986	Vancouver Centennial (UNC)	4.50
1987	Davis Strait (PR)	6.00
1987	Davis Strait (UNC)	4.50
1988	Sainte-Maurice Ironworks(PR)	8.00
1988	Sainte-Maurice Ironworks (UNC)	5.50

CASED SILVER DOLLARS

1989 MacKenzie River

Common Obverse 1990 - 2003

1990 Henry Kelsey Tricentennial

1991 Frontenac

1992 Kingston Stagecoach

1993 Stanley Cup

1994 R.C.M.P. Northern Dog Team Patrol

1995 325th Anniv. Founding of Hudson's Bay Co.

1996 200th Anniversary John McIntosh

Date	Description	Buying Price
1989	MacKenzie River (PR)	9.00
1989	MacKenzie River (UNC)	5.00
1990	Henry Kelsey (PR)	6.00
1990	Henry Kelsey (UNC)	5.00
1991	Frontenac (PR)	15.00
1991	Frontenac (UNC)	5.00
1992	Kingston Stagecoach (PR)	8.00
1992	Kingston Stagecoach (UNC)	5.00

Date	Description	Buying Price
1993	Stanley Cup (PR)	7.00
1993	Stanley Cup (UNC)	7.00
1994	R.C.M.P. (PR)	15.00
1994	R.C.M.P. (UNC)	7.00
1995	Hudson's Bay (PR)	12.00
1995	Hudson's Bay (UNC)	7.00
1996	McIntosh (PR)	18.00
1996	McIntosh (UNC)	7.00

CASED SILVER DOLLARS

1997 Canada/Russia Hockey

1997 Flying Loon

1998 125th Anniversary RCMP

1999 225th Anniv. Juan Perez

1999 Int'l Year Older Persons

2000 Voyage of Discovery

2001 50th Anniversary
National Ballet of Canada

2001 90th Anniversary
Canada's 1911 Silver Dollar

2002 50th Anniv. Elizabeth II's
Accession to the Throne

Date	Description	Buying Price
1997	Hockey (PR)	15.00
1997	Hockey (UNC)	6.00
1997	Flying Loon (PR)	80.00
1998	RCMP (PR)	14.00
1998	RCMP (UNC)	7.00
1999	Perez (PR)	18.00
1999	Perez (UNC)	7.00
1999	Older Persons (PR)	28.00

Date	Description	Buying Price
2000	Voyage of Discovery (PR)	18.00
2000	Voyage of Discovery (UNC)	7.00
2001	National Ballet of Canada (PR)	12.00
2001	National Ballet of Canada (UNC)	7.00
2001	90th Anniv. 1911 Silver Dollar (PR)	10.00
2002	50th Anniv. Accession (PR)	15.00
2002	50th Anniv. Accession (UNC)	7.00

Note: **(PR)** Proof condition one dollar silver coins are issued in a black leatherette case.
(UNC) UNC condition one dollar silver coins are issued in a clear plastic case.

CASED SILVER DOLLARS

2002 Queen Mother

2003 Cobalt

Common Obv. 2003 to 2006

2003 50th Anniv. Coronation

2004 First French Settlement

2004 The Poppy

2005 40th Anniv. Canadian Flag

2006 150th Anniv. Victoria Cross

2007 Medal of Bravery

Date	Description	Buying Price
2002	Queen Mother (PR)	250.00
2003	Cobalt (PR)	17.00
2003	Cobalt (Unc)	10.00
2003	Coronation (PR)	25.00
2004	First French Settlement (PR)	20.00
2004	First French Settlement (Unc)	10.00
2004	First French Settle. Privy Mark	60.00
2004	Lucky Loon (PR)	35.00
2004	Poppy (PR)	20.00

Date	Description	Buying Price
2005	40th Anniv. Can. Flag (PR)	24.00
2005	40th Anniv. Can. Flag (Unc)	14.00
2005	40th Anniv. Can. Flag (En.)	250.00
2006	Victoria Cross (PR)	25.00
2006	Victoria Cross (Unc)	15.00
2006	Victoria Cross (Gold Plated)	40.00
2006	Medal of Bravery (PR)	35.00
2006	Medal of Bravery (En.)	190.00

Note: (PR) Proof
(Unc) Uncirculated
(En.) Enamelled

2007 Obverse

2007 Thayendanegna

2007 Medal of Bravery

Date	Description	Buying Price
2007	Thayendanegea (PR)	25.00
2007	Thayendanegea (Unc)	15.00

Date	Description	Buying Price
2007L	Celebration of the Arts (PR)	25.00

SILVER LOON DOLLARS

Common Obv.
2004-2006

2004 Lucky Loonie

2006 Lucky Loonie

2006 Lullabies Loonie

2006 Obverse with
Maple Leaf Logo

2006 Snowflake

2007 Loon

Date	Description	Buying Price
2004	Lucky Loonie (PR)	30.00
2006	Lucky Loonie (PR)	25.00
2006	Lullabies Loonie (PR)	20.00

Date	Description	Buying Price
2006	Snowflake	20.00
2007	10th Anniv. Loon, Silver	20.00

BRONZE DOLLARS

Common obv. 1992-1997

1992 125th Anniv.

1994 Remembrance

1995 Peacekeeping

1997 Flying Loon

2002 Family of Loons

2002 Centre Ice

Common obv. 2004-2006

2004 Canada Goose

2004 Elusive Loon

2005 Puffin

2006 Snowy Owl

2007 Common Obv.

2007 Trumpeter Swan

2008 Lucky Loonie

2010 Lucky Loonie

Date	Description	Buying Price
1992	125th Anniv. of Canada	4.00
1994	Remembrance	4.00
1995	Peacekeeping	4.00
1997	Flying Loon	25.00
2002	Family of Loons	15.00
2002	Centre Ice	15.00
2004	Canada Goose	25.00

Date	Description	Buying Price
2005	Elusive Loon	20.00
2005	Tufted Puffin	20.00
2006	Snowy Owl	25.00
2007	Trumpeter Swan	10.00
2008	Luckie Loonie	10.00
2010	Luckie Loonie	10.00

Note: The bronze dollars of 1992-2010 are issued in specimen or proof sets.

TWO DOLLARS

1996 Polar Bear

ELIZABETH II 1996

Date	Description	Buying Price
1996	Proof	5.00
1996	Piedfort	50.00
1996	Gold	130.00

1999 Nunavut - Ring

1999 Nunavut - No Ring

ELIZABETH II 1999

Date	Description	Buying Price
1999	Silver	10.00
1999	Gold	125.00
1999	Mule, No Ring	125.00

2000 Polar Bears

ELIZABETH II 2000

Date	Description	Buying Price
2000	Proof	15.00
2000	Silver	15.00
2000	Gold	115.00

2004 Polar Bear, Silver

ELIZABETH II 2004

Date	Description	Buying Price
2004	Polar Bear, Silver	20.00

2006 Gold

ELIZABETH II 2006

Date	Description	Buying Price
2006	10th Anniv. Gold Two Dollar	250.00

THREE DOLLARS

THE BEAVER (Square)

Date	Description	Buying Price
2006	The Beaver	50.00

FIVE DOLLAR COINS

1998 Bethune

Canada $5

China

1999 Viking Settlement

Canada $5

Norway 20 Kroner

2001 Marconi

Canada $5

British £2

2003 F.I.F.A. World Cup

Date	Description	Buying Price
1998	Bethune, 2 coin set	30.00
1999	Viking Settlement, 2 coin set	30.00

Date	Description	Buying Price
2001	Marconi, 2 coin set	20.00
2004	World Cup	20.00

FIVE DOLLAR COINS

Common obv. (except for date) 2004-2005

2004 100th Anniversary Canadian Open Championship

2004 Majestic Moose

2005 60th Anniversary of the end of the Second World War

Common obv. 2005-2006

2005 Alberta Centennial

2005 Saskatchewan Centennial

Obverse 2006

2006 Breast Cancer

Date	Description	Buying Price
2004	100th Anniv. Canadian Open Golf	15.00
2004	Majestic Moose	100.00
2005	60th Anniv., RCM Rev.	15.00

Date	Description	Buying Price
2005	Alberta Centennial	20.00
2005	Saskatchewan Centennial	20.00
2006	Breast Cancer	30.00

FIVE DOLLAR COIN

Common obv. 2005-2006

2005 White-tailed Deer and Fawn

2005 Atlantic Walrus and Calf

2006 Peregrine Falcon and Nestlings

2006 Sable Island Horse and Foal

2006 Snowbirds

Date	Description	Buying Price
2005	White-tailed Deer and Fawn	30.00
2005	Atlantic Walrus and Calf	25.00
2006	Peregrine Falcon and Nestlings	25.00

Date	Description	Buying Price
2006	Sable Island Horse and Foal	25.00
2006	Snowbirds	30.00

FIVE AND TEN DOLLAR COINS
1976 MONTREAL OLYMPIC COINS

For the Summer Olympic Games of 1976, held in Montreal, seven series of silver coins were minted. There were four different coins in each series. Two $5.00 and two $10.00 coins, struck in sterling silver. The $5.00 coins weigh 24.3 grams and the $10.00 coins weigh 48.6 grams. The coins were available, encapsulated in plastic, as single coins, and in custom, prestige and proof four-coin sets. Each set of four coins, with a face value of $30.00, contains 4.28 oz. of fine silver. The purchase price of these sets is linked to the market price of silver, even if the intrinsic value falls below the face value. Large quantities of these coins were issued, and they are not redeemable by the government or the banks.

SERIES I

$5 Map of North America

$5 Kingston

$10 World Map

$10 Montreal

SERIES II

$5 Athlete with Torch

$5 Olive Wreath

FIVE AND TEN DOLLAR COINS

$10 Head of Zeus

$10 Temple of Zeus

SERIES III

$5 Canoeing

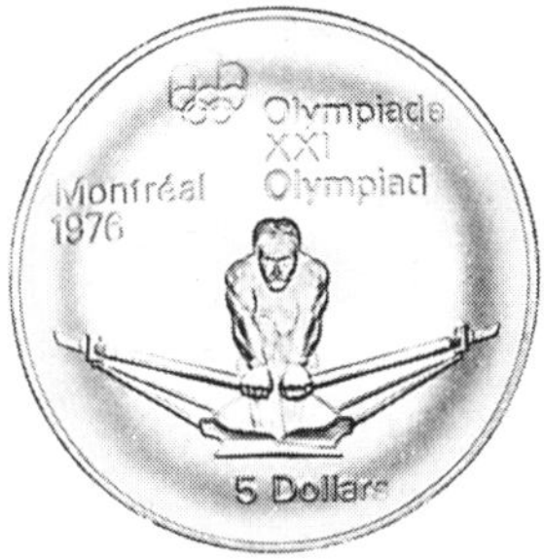

$5 Rowing

$10 Lacrosse

$10 Bicycling

SERIES IV

$5 The Marathon

$5 Ladies' Javelin

FIVE AND TEN DOLLAR COINS

$10 Men's Hurdles

$10 Ladies' Shot Put

SERIES V

$5 The Diver

$5 The Swimmer

$10 The Paddler

$10 Sailing

SERIES VI

$5 Fencing

$5 Boxing

FIVE AND TEN DOLLAR COINS

$10 Field Hockey

$10 Football

SERIES VII

$5 Olympic Flame

$5 Oylmpic Village

$10 Olympic Stadium

$10 Olympic Velodrome

Date	Series	$5 Coin	$10 Coin	Custom Set	Prestige Set	Proof Set
1973	1	9.00	18.00	54.00	54.00	65.00
1974	Mule	–	150.00			
1974	2	9.00	18.00	54.00	54.00	65.00
1974	3	9.00	18.00	54.00	54.00	65.00
1975	4	9.00	18.00	54.00	54.00	65.00
1975	5	9.00	18.00	54.00	54.00	65.00
1976	6	9.00	18.00	54.00	54.00	65.00
1976	7	9.00	18.00	54.00	54.00	65.00

EIGHT DOLLAR COINS

2004 Obv.

2004 Great Grizzly

2005 Railway Bridge

Elizabeth II 2004-2005

2005 Chinese Memorial

SHAPE OF TRADE IN CHINA, 2007

Obverse

Reverse

Date	Description	Buying Price
2004	Great Grizzly	50.00
2005	Railway Bridge	25.00
2005	Chinese Memorial	25.00
2007	Trade in Ancient China	25.00

TEN DOLLAR COINS

2005 Year of the Veteran

2006 Pope John Paul II

2006 Fortress of Louisbourg

Date	Description	Buying Price
2005	Year of the Veteran	25.00
2006	Pope John Paul II	25.00

Date	Description	Buying Price
2006	Fortress of Louisbourg	25.00

FIFTEEN DOLLAR COINS
Olympic Centennial Coins

Olympic Sports Reverse
Speed Skater, Pole Vaulter,
Gymnast

Olympic Spirit Reverse

Date	Description	Buying Price
1992	Sports	20.00

Date	Description	Buying Price
1992	Spirit of the Generations	20.00

FIFTEEN DOLLAR COINS
Chinese Lunar Calender Coins

1998 The Year of the Tiger

1999 The Year of the Rabbit

2000 The Year of the Dragon

2001 The Year of the Snake

2002 The Year of the Horse

2003 The Year of the Ram

2004 The Year of the Monkey

2005 The Year of the Rooster

2006 Year of the Dog

Date	Description	Buying Price	Date	Description	Buying Price
1998	Tiger	300.00	2003	Ram	40.00
1999	Rabbit	30.00	2004	Monkey	60.00
2000	Dragon	85.00	2005	Rooster	55.00
2001	Snake	35.00	2006	Dog	45.00
2002	Horse	40.00	2007	Pig	40.00

TWENTY DOLLAR COINS
CALGARY OLYMPIC GAMES

The XV Winter Olympic Games were held in Calgary, February 13th to 29th, 1988. Ten different $20 silver coins were issued to commemorate this event. The coins weigh 34.107 grams, the composition is .925 silver and .075 copper, and they were issued in proof singles or proof sets in one or two coin display cases. Incorporated into the design of these coins are the letters "XV OLYMPIC WINTER GAMES - XVes JEUX OLYMPIQUE D'HIVER" impressed into the edge. During the striking of these coins at the Royal Canadian Mint, the impressed procedures were skipped on some series resulting in the edge lettering being missed on four known coins, resulting in varieties.

FIRST SERIES

Downhill Skiing

Speed Skating

SECOND SERIES

Hockey

Biathalon

THIRD SERIES

Cross-Country Skiing

Free-Style Skiing

TWENTY DOLLAR COINS

FOURTH SERIES

Figure Skating

Curling

FIFTH SERIES

Ski Jumping

Bobsleigh

Date	Description	Buying Single	Buying Set
1985	Downhill Skiiing	20.00	
1985	Speed Skating	20.00	40.00
1985	Speed Skating, no edge lettering	100.00	
1986	Hockey	20.00	
1986	Hockey, no edge lettering	100.00	
1986	Biathalon	20.00	40.00
1986	Biathalon, no edge lettering	100.00	
1986	Cross-Country Skiing	20.00	
1986	Free-Style Skiing	20.00	40.00
1986	Free-Style Skiing, no edge lettering	100.00	
1987	Figure Skating	20.00	
1987	Curling	20.00	40.00
1987	Ski Jumping	20.00	
1987	Bobsleigh	20.00	40.00

TWENTY DOLLAR COINS

AVIATION FIRST SERIES 1990 - 1994

Canada's aviation heroes and their achievements are commemorated on this first series of twenty dollar sterling-silver coins. The series is made up of ten coins, which were issued two per year over five years. For the first time, each coin design contains a 24-karat-gold-covered oval cameo portrait of the aviation hero commemorated. A maximum of 50,000 of each coin was offered for sale.

Coin No. 1
Anson and Harvard /
Robert Leckie

Coin No. 2
Avro Lancaster /
J. E. Fauquier

Coin No. 3
A. E. A. Silver Dart / F. W. Baldwin
and J. A. D. McCurdy

Coin No. 4
de Havilland Beaver /
Phillip C. Garratt

Coin No. 5
Curtiss JN-4 (Canuck) /
Sir F. W. Baillie

Coin No. 6
de Havilland Gypsy Moth /
Murton A. Seymour

TWENTY DOLLAR COINS

AVIATION FIRST SERIES 1990 - 1994 (cont.)

Coin No. 7
Fairchild 71C / J. A. Richardson

Coin No. 8
Super Electra / Z. L. Leigh

Coin No. 9
Curtiss HS-2L / Stuart Graham

Coin No. 10
Vickers Vedette / T. Reid

Date	Coin No.	Description	Buying Price
1990	1	Anson and Harvard / Leckie	25.00
1990	2	Lancaster / Fauquier	60.00
1991	3	Silver Dart / Baldwin, McCurdy	25.00
1991	4	Beaver / Garratt	25.00
1992	5	Curtiss / Baille	25.00
1992	6	Gypsy Moth / Seymour	25.00
1993	7	Fairchild / Richardson	25.00
1993	8	Super Electra / Leigh	25.00
1994	9	Curtiss / Graham	25.00
1994	10	Vedette / Reid	25.00

TWENTY DOLLAR COINS

AVIATION SECOND SERIES 1995 - 1999

This second series of aviation coins celebrates "Powered Flight in Canada – Beyond World War II." As with the first series, it was made up of ten coins to be issued two per year over five years. Each coin design contains a 24-karat-gold-covered oval cameo portrait of the pilot, engineers or designers of the aircrafts. A maximum of 50,000 of each coin was offered for sale.

Coin No. 11
The Fleet 80 Canuck / Noury

Coin No. 12
DHC-1 Chipmunk / Bannock

Coin No. 13
CF-100 Canuck / Zurakowski

Coin No. 14
CF-105 Arrow / Chamberlain

Date	Coin No.	Description	Buying Price
1995	11	Fleet 80 Canuck / Noury	25.00
1995	12	DHC-1 Chipmunk / Bannock	25.00
1996	13	CF-100 Canuck / Zurakowski	25.00
1996	14	CF-105 Arrow / Chamberlin	60.00

TWENTY DOLLAR COINS

AVIATION SECOND SERIES 1995 - 1999 (cont.)

Coin No. 15
Canadian F-86 Sabre /
Fern Villeneuve

Coin No. 16
Canadair CT-114 Tutor /
Edward Higgins

Coin No. 17
CP-107 Argus /
William S. Longhurst

Coin No. 18
CL-215 Waterbomber /
Paul Gagnon

Coin No. 19
DHC-6 Twin Otter / G. A. Neal

Coin No. 20
DHC-8 Dash 8 / R. H. Fowler

Date	Coin No.	Description	Buying Price
1997	15	F-86 Sabre / Villeneuve	25.00
1997	16	CT-114 Tutor / Higgin	25.00
1998	17	CP-107 Argus / Longhurst	25.00
1998	18	CL-215 Waterbomber / Gagnon	30.00
1999	19	DHC-6 Twin Otter / Neal	40.00
1999	20	DHC-8 Dash 8 / Fowler	40.00

TWENTY DOLLAR COINS

LAND, SEA AND RAIL 2000 - 2002

Coin No. 1
H. S. Taylor Steam Buggy

Coin No. 2
The Bluenose

Coin No. 3
The Toronto

Coin No. 4
The Russel

Coin No. 5
The Marco Polo

Coin No. 6
The Scotia

Coin No. 7
The Gray-Dort

Coin No. 8
The William Lawrence

Coin No. 9
The D-10 Locomotive

Date	Coin No.	Description	Buying Price
2000	1	H. S. Taylor Steam Buggy	30.00
2000	2	The Bluenose	100.00
2000	3	The Toronto	30.00
2001	4	The Russel	30.00
2001	5	The Marco Polo	30.00
2001	6	The Scotia	30.00
2002	7	The Gray-Dort	30.00
2002	8	The William Lawrence	30.00
2002	9	The D-10 Locomotive	30.00

TWENTY DOLLAR COINS

LAND, SEA AND RAIL 2003

Coin No. 10
HMCS Bras d'or

Coin No. 11
CNR FA-1 Diesel Electric

Coin No. 12
Bricklin SV-1

Date	Coin No.	Description	Buying Price
2003	10	HMCS Bras d'or	30.00
2003	11	C.N.R. FA-1 Diesel Electric Locomotive	40.00
2003	12	Bricklin SV-1	35.00

NATURAL WONDERS COLLECTION

Coin No. 1 Niagara Falls

Coin No. 2 Rocky Mountains

Coin No. 3 Icebergs

Coin No. 4 Northern Lights

Coin No. 5 Hopewell Rocks

Coin No. 6 Diamonds

Date	Coin No.	Description	Buying Price
2003	1	Niagara Falls	45.00
2003	2	Rocky Mountains	35.00
2004	3	Icebergs	35.00
2004	4	Northern Lights	40.00
2005	5	Hopewell Rocks	35.00
2005	6	Diamonds	35.00

TWENTY DOLLAR COINS

TALL SHIPS COLLECTION

Coin No. 1 Three-Masted Ship

Coin No. 2 Ketch

Coin No. 3 Brigantine

Date	Coin No.	Description	Buying Price
2005	1	Three-masted Ship, Hologram	35.00
2006	2	Ketch, Hologram	35.00
2007	3	Brigantine, Hologram	35.00

NATIONAL PARKS SERIES

Coin No. 1
North Pacific
Rim

Coin No. 2
Mingan
Archipelago

Coin No. 3 Georgian Bay

Coin No. 4 Nahanni Park

Coin No. 5 Jasper National Park

Date	Coin No.	Description	Buying Price
2005	1	North Pacific Rim National Park Reserve	35.00
2005	2	Mingan Archipelago National Park Reserve	35.00
2006	3	Georgian Bay Islands National Park	35.00
2006	4	Nahanni National Park Reserve	35.00
2006	5	Jasper National Park	35.00

TWENTY DOLLAR COINS

CANADIAN ARCHITECTURAL COLLECTION

Coin No. 1 Notre Dame Basilica

Coin No. 2 CN Tower

Coin No. 3 Pengrowth Saddledome

Date	Coin No.	Description	Buying Price
2006	1	Notre Dame Basilica, Hologram	35.00
2006	2	30th Anniversary CN Tower, Hologram	35.00
2006	3	Pengrowth Saddledome, Hologram	35.00

TWENTY FIVE DOLLARS

VANCOUVER WINTER OLYMPICS

Coin. No. 1 Curling

Coin No. 2 Ice Hockey

Date	Coin No.	Description	Buying Price
2007	1	Curling	35.00
2007	2	Ice Hockey	35.00

THIRTY DOLLAR COINS

Welcome Figure Totem Pole

5th Anniversary Canadarm

Dog Sled

National War Memorial

Beaumont-Hamel Newfoundland Memorial

Canadian National Vimy Memorial

Date	Description	Buying Price
2006	Welcome Figure Totem Pole	40.00
2006	5th Anniversary Canadarm	40.00
2006	Dog Sled	40.00
2006	National War Memorial	40.00
2006	Beaumont-Hamel Newfoundland Memorial	40.00
2007	Canadian National Vimy Memorial	40.00

FIFTY DOLLAR COIN

THE FOUR SEASONS

Date	Description	Buying Price
2006	The Four Seasons	150.00

TWO HUNDRED FIFTY DOLLAR COIN

VANCOUVER WINTER OLYMPICS

Date	Description	Buying Price
2007	Early Canada	500.00

Note: Coins illustrated smaller than actual size.

ONE DOLLAR GOLD COIN

Date	Description	Buying Price
2006	Gold Louis	50.00

TWENTY DOLLAR GOLD COIN

Date	Description	Buying Price
1967	Centennial Confederation	280.00

50 DOLLAR GOLD COIN

Date	Description	Buying Price
2005	60th Anniv. End WWII	160.00

SEVENTY FIVE DOLLAR COINS

Pope John Paul II

2007 Common Obv.

2007 R.C.M.P.

2007 Athlete's Pride

2007 Canada Geese

Date	Description	Buying Price
2005	Pope John Paul II	300.00
2007	R.C.M.P.	200.00
2007	Athlete's Pride	200.00
2007	Canada Geese	200.00

ONE HUNDRED DOLLAR GOLD COINS

Canada issued the first one-hundred-dollar gold coin in 1976 to commemorate the Montreal Olympic Games. In that year two qualities and proportions of fineness were released; uncirculated coins were .585 fine (14 karat), and proof coins were .916 fine (22 karat). From 1976 to 1986, only proof quality coins with a fineness of .916 were issued. In 1987 the quality remained the same (proof), but the fineness of the coin was altered to .583 fine, or 14 karat, again.

IMPORTANT

Proof coins must be in mint-state condition. Mishandled, mounted or damaged coins are discounted from the prices listed. The buying price for gold coins is tied to the market price of gold. Any movement in the gold price will result in a corresponding price movement for these coins.

1976 - 14kt

1976 - 22 kt

1977

1978

1979

1980

1981

1982

1983

1984

Date	Description	Fineness	Buying Price
1976	14 kt Olympic	.583	140.00
1976	22 kt Olympic	.916	280.00
1977	Jubilee	.916	280.00
1978	Unity	.916	280.00
1979	Year of the Child	.916	280.00
1980	Arctic Territories	.916	280.00
1981	"O Canada"	.916	280.00
1982	Constitution	.916	280.00
1983	Gilbert's Landing	.916	280.00
1984	Voyage of Discovery	.916	280.00

ONE HUNDRED DOLLAR GOLD COINS

1985

1986

1987

1988

1989

1990

1991

1992

1993

1994

1995

1996

1997

1998

1999

2000

Date	Description	Fineness	Buying Price
1985	National Parks	.916	280.00
1986	Peace	.916	280.00
1987	Calgary Olympics	.583	140.00
1988	Bowhead Whale	.583	140.00
1989	Ste. Marie	.583	140.00
1990	Literacy Year	.583	140.00
1991	Empress of India	.583	140.00
1992	Montreal	.583	140.00
1993	Horseless Carriage	.583	140.00
1994	The Home Front	.583	140.00
1995	Louisbourg	.583	140.00
1996	Klondike Gold Rush	.583	140.00
1997	Bell	.583	140.00
1998	Insulin	.583	140.00
1999	Newfoundland	.583	190.00
2000	Northwest Passage	.583	190.00

ONE HUNDRED DOLLAR GOLD COINS

2001

2002

2003

2004

2005

2006

2007

Date	Description	Fineness	Buying Price
2001	Library	.583	190.00
2002	Oil Well	.583	300.00
2003	Wheat	.583	180.00
2004	Seaway	.583	200.00
2005	Supreme Court	.583	200.00
2006	Hockey	.583	200.00
2007	140th Anniv.	.583	200.00

150 DOLLAR GOLD COINS

2000

2001

2002

2003

2004

2005

2006

2007

Date	Description	Fineness	Buying Price
2000	Year of the Dragon	.750	675.00
2001	Year of the Snake	.750	200.00
2002	Year of the Horse	.750	225.00
2003	Year of the Ram	.750	225.00
2004	Year of the Monkey	.750	300.00
2005	Year of the Rooster	.750	250.00
2006	Year of the Dog	.750	250.00
2007	Year of the Pig	.750	250.00

175 DOLLAR GOLD COIN

Date	Description	Fineness	Buying Price
1992	Olympic	.916	300.00

200 DOLLAR GOLD COINS

22 KARAT (.916) GOLD

1990

1991

1992

1993

1994

1995

1996

1997

1998

1999

2000

2001

2002

2003

2004

2005

Date	Description	Buying Price
1990	Canada Flag	280.00
1991	A National Passion	280.00
1992	Niagara Falls	280.00
1993	RCMP	280.00
1994	Anne of Green Gables	280.00
1995	Sugar Bush	280.00
1996	Transcontinental	280.00
1997	Haida	400.00

Date	Description	Buying Price
1998	White Buffalo	280.00
1999	Mikmaq Butterfly	280.00
2000	Mother and Child	300.00
2001	Cornelius Krieghoff	300.00
2002	Tom Thomson	300.00
2003	Lionel Fitzgerald	300.00
2004	Alfred Pellan	300.00
2005	Fur Traders	300.00

200 DOLLAR GOLD COINS

22 KARAT (.916) GOLD

2006

2007

Date	Description	Buying Price
2006	Timber Trade	300.00
2007	Fishing Trade	300.00

250 DOLLAR GOLD COINS

14 KARAT (.583) GOLD

2006 Obv.

2006 Dog Sled Team

Date	Description	Buying Price
2006	Dog Sled Team	300.00

300 DOLLAR GOLD COINS

14 KARAT (.583) GOLD, LARGE SIZE (50 mm)

2002 Jubilee / Triple Cameo

2003 Great Seal of Canada

2004 Arms of Canada / Quadruple Cameo

2005 The 1870 Shinplaster

2006 The 1900 Shinplaster

2006 The 1923 Shinplaster

Date	Description	Buying Price
2002	Jubilee / Triple Cameo Portraits	825.00
2003	Great Seal of Canada	825.00
2004	Quadruple Cameo Portraits	825.00

Date	Description	Buying Price
2005	The 1870 Shinplaster	825.00
2006	The 1900 Shinplaster	825.00
2007	The 1923 Shinplaster	825.00

300 DOLLAR GOLD COINS

14 KARAT (.583) GOLD, LARGE SIZE (50 mm)

2006 Crystal Snowflake

2006 80th Birthday Queen Elizabeth II

2007 Olympic Ideals

2008 Competition

Date	Description	Buying Price
2006	Snowflake	825.00
2006	80th Birthday Elizabeth II	825.00
2007	Olympic Ideals	825.00
2008	Olympic Competition	825.00

300 DOLLAR GOLD COINS

14 KARAT (.583) GOLD, SMALL SIZE (40 mm)

Pacific Time 4:00

Mountain Time 5:00

Central Time 6:00

Eastern Time 7:00

Atlantic Time 8:00

Newfoundland Time 8:30

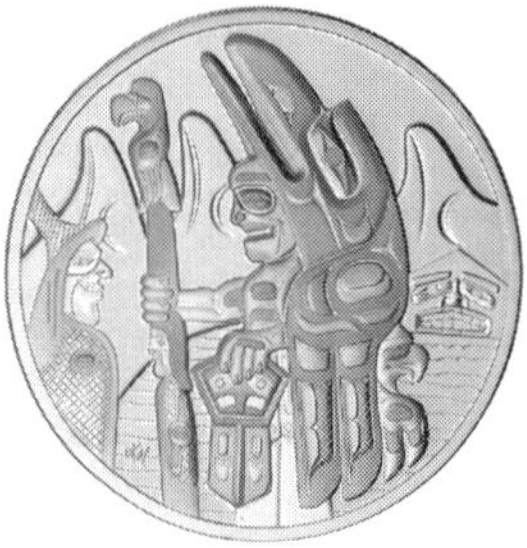

Welcome Figure Totem Pole

5th Anniv. Canadarm

Date	Description	Buying Price
2005	Pacific Time 4:00	650.00
2005	Mountain Time 5:00	650.00
2005	Central Time 6:00	650.00
2005	Eastern Time 7:00	650.00
2005	Atlantic Time 8:00	650.00
2005	Newfoundland Time 8:30	650.00
2005	Welcome Figure Totem Pole	650.00
2006	5th Anniv. Canadarm	650.00

Note: Images on page 90, 91 and 92 shown smaller than actual size.

350 DOLLAR GOLD COINS
24 Karat (.99999) GOLD

Obv. 1998-2003

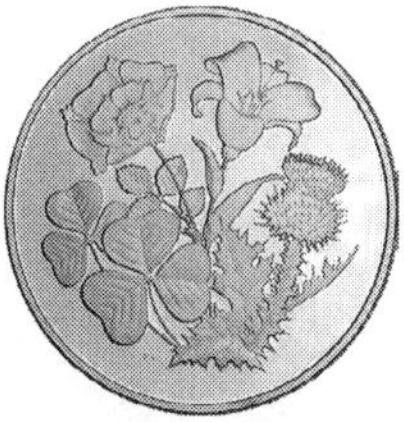
1998

1999

2000

2001

2002

2003

Obv. 2004-2006

2004

2005

2006

Obv. 2007

2007

Date	Description	Buying Price
1998	90th Anniv. R.C.M.	950.00
1999	Golden Slipper	850.00
2000	Pacific Dogwood	850.00
2001	Mayflower	850.00
2002	Wild Rose	850.00
2003	Trillium	850.00
2004	Fireweed	850.00
2005	Western Red Lily	850.00
2006	Iris Versicolor	850.00
2007	Purple Violet	850.00

PALLADIUM COINS

FIFTY DOLLARS

BIG AND LITTLE BEAR CONSTELLATIONS, 2006

Spring

Summer

Autumn

Winter

Date	Description	Buying Price
2006	Spring	400.00
2006	Summer	400.00
2006	Autumn	400.00
2006	Winter	400.00

PROOF PLATINUM COINS

1990 Polar Bears

1991 Snowy Owls

1992 Cougars

1993 Arctic Foxes

1994 Otters

1995 Canada Lynx

1996 Peregrine Falcon

1997 Wood Bison

1998 Grey Wolf

1999 Muskox

2000 Pronghorn

2001 Harlequin Duck

2002 Great Blue Heron

2003 Atlantic Walrus

2004 Grizzly Bear

Date	Description	Buying Price
1990	Polar Bear Set	2,150.00
1991	Snowy Owl Set	2,150.00
1992	Cougar Set	2,150.00
1993	Arctic Foxes Set	2,150.00
1994	Sea Otters Set	2,150.00
1995	Canada Lynx Set	2,150.00
1995	Canada Lynx $30	110.00
1995	Canada Lynx $150	550.00
1996	Peregrine Falcon Set	2,150.00
1996	Peregrine Falcon $30	110.00
1996	Peregrine Falcon $50	550.00
1997	Wood Bison Set	2,150.00
1997	Wood Bison $30	110.00
1997	Wood Bison $150	550.00
1998	Grey Wolf Set	2,150.00
1998	Grey Wolf $30	110.00
1998	Grey Wolf $150	550.00
1999	Muskox Set	2,150.00
1999	Muskox $30	110.00
2000	Pronghorn Set	2,150.00
2001	Harlequin Duck Set	2,150.00
2002	Great Blue Heron Set	2,150.00
2003	Atlantic Walrus Set	2,150.00
2004	Grizzly Bear Set	2,150.00

Note: The Platinum Proof Set contains four coins: $300., $150., $75. and $30. coins.

COLLECTOR SETS

Listed on this and the following page are the Collector sets of coins issued by the Royal Canadian Mint between the years 1954 and 2005.

SIX COIN PROOF-LIKE AND BRILLIANT UNCIRCULATED SETS

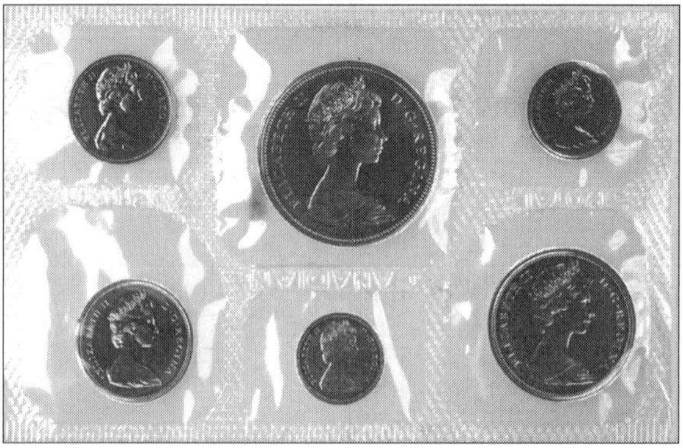

SILVER 6-COIN PROOF-LIKE SETS

Date	Description	Buying Price
1954	Voyageur	300.00
1955	Voyageur	200.00
1955	Arnprior	325.00
1956	Voyageur	125.00
1957	Voyageur	75.00
1958	British Columbia	65.00
1959	Voyageur	30.00
1960	Voyageur	12.50
1961	Voyageur	12.50
1962	Voyageur	12.50
1963	Voyageur	12.50
1964	Charlottetown	12.50
1965	Voyageur	12.50
1966	Voyageur	12.50
1967	Centennial	12.50

NICKEL 6-COIN BRILLIANT UNCIRCULATED SETS

Date	Description	Buying Price
1968	Voyageur	2.00
1969	Voyageur	2.00
1970	Manitoba	2.00
1971	British Columbia	2.00
1972	Voyageur	2.00
1973	R.C.M.P., Small Bust	2.00
1973	R.C.M.P., Large Bust	150.00
1974	Winnipeg	2.00
1975	Voyageur	2.00
1976	Voyageur	2.00
1977	Voyageur	2.00
1978	Voyageur	2.00
1979	Voyageur	2.00
1980	Voyageur	2.00
1981	Voyageur	2.00
1982	Voyageur	2.00
1983	Voyageur	3.00
1984	Voyageur	3.00
1985	Voyageur	3.00
1986	Voyageur	3.00
1987	Voyageur	3.00
1988	Loon	3.00
1989	Loon	5.00
1990	Loon	5.00
1991	Loon	15.00
1992	Loon	6.00
1993	Loon	3.00
1994	Loon	4.00
1995	Loon	4.00
1996	Loon	15.00

BRILLIANT UNCIRCULATED SETS

NICKEL 7-COIN SETS

Date	Description	Buying Price
1997	Loon/Polar Bear	5.00
1998W	Loon/Polar Bear	10.00
1998	Loon/Polar Bear	8.00
1999	Loon/Polar Bear	6.00
1999	Loon/Nunavut	8.00
2000	Loon/Polar Bear	7.00
2000W	Loon/Polar Bear	7.00
2000	Loon/Polar Bears	7.00

PLATED STEEL 7-COIN SETS

Date	Description	Buying Price
2001P	Loon/Polar Bear	8.00
1952-2002P	Loon/Polar Bear	9.00
1952-2002P	Special	9.00
2003P	Loon/Polar Bear	12.00
2003WP	Special	10.00
2004P	Loon/Polar Bear	12.00
2005P	Loon/Polar Bear	11.00
2006P	Loon/Polar Bear	11.00
2007L	Loon/Polar Bear	11.00

"OH CANADA!", BUNDLE OF JOY, and TINY TREASURES SETS

"OH CANADA!" NICKEL 6-COIN SETS

Date	Description	Buying Price
1994	Loon	6.00
1995	Peacekeeping	4.00
1996	Loon	8.00

"OH CANADA!" NICKEL 7-COIN SETS

Date	Description	Buying Price
1997	Flying Loon/Polar Bear	17.00
1998	Loon/Polar Bear	8.00
1998W	Loon/Polar Bear	10.00
1999	Loon/Polar Bear	7.00
2000	Loon/Polar Bear	7.00
2000W	Loon/Polar Bear	7.00

"OH CANADA!" MULTI-PLY PLATED STEEL 7-COIN SETS

Date	Description	Buying Price
2001P	Loon/Polar Bear	7.00
2002P	Loon/Polar Bear	8.00
2003P	Loon/Polar Bear	9.00
2004P	Loon/Polar Bear	11.00
2005P	Loon/Polar Bear	10.00
2006P	Loon/Polar Bear	10.00
2007L	Loon/Polar Bear	10.00

"BUNDLE OF JOY/TINY TREASURES" NICKEL 6-COIN SETS

Date	Description	Buying Price
1995	Loon	9.00
1996	Loon	9.00

"BUNDLE OF JOY/TINY TREASURES" NICKEL 7-COIN SETS

Date	Description	Buying Price
1997	Loon/Polar Bear	8.00
1998	Loon/Polar Bear	8.00
1998W	Loon/Polar Bear	10.00
1999	Loon/Polar Bear	8.00
2000	Loon/Polar Bear	7.00
2000W	Loon/Polar Bear	7.00
2001	Loon/Polar Bears	7.00

"GIFT SETS" MULTI-PLY PLATED STEEL 7-COIN SETS

Date	Description	Buying Price
2001P	Loon/Polar Bear	7.00
2002P	Loon/Polar Bear	8.00
2003P	Loon/Polar Bear	11.00
2004P	Loon/Polar Bear	11.00
2005P	Loon/Polar Bear	10.00
2006P	Loon/Polar Bear	10.00
2007L	Loon/Polar Bear	10.00

SPECIAL EDITION BRILLIANT UNCIRCULATED SETS

7-COIN SETS

Date	Description	Buying Price
2002P	Accession	9.00
2003WP	Coronation	10.00
2006L	10th Anniversary	10.00

8-COIN SETS

Date	Description	Buying Price
2005P	Alberta Centenary	11.00
2005P	Saskatchewan Centenary	11.00

11-COIN SETS

Date	Description	Buying Price
2007L	Winter Olympics	10.00

SPECIMEN SETS

SPECIMEN 7-COIN SETS

Date	Description	Buying Price
1971	Voyageur	3.00
1972	Voyageur	3.00
1973	Voyageur/RCMP, Small Bust	3.00
1973	Voyageur/RCMP, Large Bust	125.00
1974	Voyaguer	3.00
1975	Voyageur	3.00
1976	Voyageur	3.00
1977	Voyageur	3.00
1978	Voyageur	3.00
1979	Voyageur	3.00
1980	Voyageur	3.00

6-COIN SETS

Date	Description	Buying Price
1981	Voyageur	3.50
1982	Voyageur	3.50
1983	Voyageur	3.50
1984	Voyageur	3.50
1985	Voyageur	3.50
1986	Voyageur	3.50
1987	Voyageur	3.50
1988	Loon	3.50
1989	Loon	4.00

SPECIMEN 6-COIN SETS (cont.)

Date	Description	Buying Price
1990	Loon	4.00
1991	Loon	17.00
1992	Loon	7.00
1993	Loon	5.00
1994	Loon	5.00
1995	Loon	5.00
1996	Loon	4.00

SPECIMEN 7-COIN SETS

Date	Description	Buying Price
1997	Flying Loon	20.00
1998	Loon/Polar Bear	8.00
1999	Loon/Polar Bear	7.00
2000	Loon/Polar Bear	7.00
2000	Loon/Polar Bears	7.00
2001P	Loon/Polar Bear	7.00
2002P	Loon Family /Polar Bear	25.00
2003P	Loon/Polar Bear	15.00
2004P	Canada Goose/Polar Bear	25.00
2005P	Puffin/Polar Bear	30.00
2006P	Snowy Owl/Polar Bear	30.00
2007L	Trumpeter Swans/ Polar Bear	30.00

PROOF SETS

PROOF 7-COIN SETS

Date	Description	Buying Price
1971	British Columbia	8.00
1972	Voyageur	20.00
1973	R.C.M.P., Small Bust	8.00
1973	R.C.M.P., Large Bust	200.00
1974	Winnipeg	8.00
1975	Calgary	8.00
1976	Parliament	8.00
1977	Jubilee	8.00
1978	Commonwealth Games	8.00
1979	Griffon	10.00
1980	Polar Bear	15.00
1981	Trans Canada	11.00
1982	Regina	10.00
1983	University Games	10.00
1984	Toronto	12.00
1985	National Parks	14.00
1986	Vancouver	13.00
1987	Davis Straits	13.00
1988	Ironworks	15.00
1989	MacKenzie River	15.00
1990	Henry Kelsey	15.00

PROOF 7-COIN SETS

Date	Description	Buying Price
1991	Frontenac	30.00
1992	Stagecoach	20.00
1993	Hockey	16.00
1994	RCMP	15.00
1994	RCMP Red Box	15.00
1995	Hudson's Bay	15.00
1995	Hudson's Bay Red Box	15.00
1996	John McIntosh	25.00

PROOF 8-COIN SETS

Date	Description	Buying Price
1997	Canada/Russia Hockey	23.00
1998	RCMP 125th Anniversary	30.00
1999	Juan Perez	45.00
2000	Discovery	40.00
2001	Ballet	25.00
2002	Jubilee	40.00
2003	Cobalt	50.00
2004	Ste Croix	50.00
2005	Canadian Flag	60.00
2006	Victoria Cross	60.00
2007	Thayendanegea	60.00

MAPLE LEAF BULLION COINS

The Maple Leaf gold coins were first produced in 1979, the fractional or small sizes three years later in 1982, and the half-ounce size in 1986. In 1988 the four sizes; $5.00, $10.00, $20.00 and $50.00, of platinum were added. Expanding the range in 1993, $1.00 gold and platinum coins were issued, and again in 1994 $2.00 coins were placed on the market.

The price of Maple Leaf bullion coins is based on the spot market price in Canadian dollars on the day of purchase, times their gold content, less a small handling charge.

$50

$20

$10

$5

COIN SPECIFICATIONS

Denomination	Description	Content	Weight Tr. Oz.
$1	1/20 Maple	Gold or platinum	.050
$2	1/15 Maple	Gold or platinum	.667
$5	1/10 Maple	Gold or platinum	.100
$10	1/4 Maple	Gold or platinum	.250
$20	1/2 Maple	Gold or platinum	.500
$50	Maple	Gold or platinum	1.00
$5	Maple	Silver	1.00
$50	10 Maple	Silver	10.00

MAPLE LEAF PROOF BULLION ISSUES OF 1989

To commemorate the tenth anniversary of the Maple Leaf bullion program, the Royal Canadian Mint, in 1989, issued a series of proof condition silver, gold and platinum coins, individually and in sets. The single coins and sets were packaged in solid maple presentation cases with brown velvet liners.

Type	Description	Buying Price
Sets	Gold 4 coins: 1, 1/2, 1/4, 1/10 ounce maple	1,300.00
	Platinum 4 coins: 1, 1/2, 1/4, 1/10 ounce maple	2,150.00
	Gold and Platinum 1/10 ounce maple each, Silver 1 ounce Maple, 3 coins	225.00
	Gold, Platinum and Silver 3 coins: 1 ounce maple each	2,100.00
Singles	Gold, One Maple	700.00
	Silver, One Maple	20.00

PAPER MONEY OF CANADA

PROVINCE OF CANADA

1866 ISSUES

Denom.	Issue Date	Buying Price
$1	1866	1,100.00
$2	1866	1,900.00
$5	1866	4,500.00

Denom.	Issue Date	Buying Price
$10	1866	7,500.00
$20	1866	10,000.00
$50	1866	15,000.00

CANADA

1870 ISSUES

Plain

Series Letter A

Series Letter B

Denom.	Issue Date	Buying Price
25-cent Plain	1870	15.00
25-cent Series A	1870	125.00

Denom.	Issue Date	Buying Price
25-cent Series B	1870	20.00

Note: The buying prices listed are for notes in **Very Good (VG)** condition.

1870 ISSUES

Denom.	Issue Date	Variety/Signature	Buying Price
$1	1870	Payable at Montreal or Toronto	500.00
$1	1870	Payable at Halifax	2,000.00
$1	1870	Payable at St. John	2,000.00
$2	1870	Payable at Montreal or Toronto	1,950.00
$2	1870	Payable at Halifax or St. John	3,500.00

1878 ISSUES

Denom.	Issue Date	Variety/Signature	Buying Price
$1	1878	Scalloped Frame, Payable at Montreal or Toronto	375.00
$1	1878	Scalloped Frame, Payable at St. John or Halifax	1,300.00
$1	1878	Lettered Frame, Payable at Montreal or Toronto	175.00
$1	1878	Lettered Frame, Payable at St. John or Halifax	1,500.00
$2	1878	Payable at Montreal or Toronto	1,375.00
$2	1878	Payable at St. John or Halifax	2,250.00

1882 AND 1887 ISSUES

Denom.	Issue Date	Variety/Signature	Buying Price
$4	1882		900.00
$2	1887	Plain,	450.00
$2	1887	Series A	2,000.00

Note: The buying prices listed are for notes in **Very Good (VG)** condition.

1897 AND 1898 ISSUES

No "One" 1897

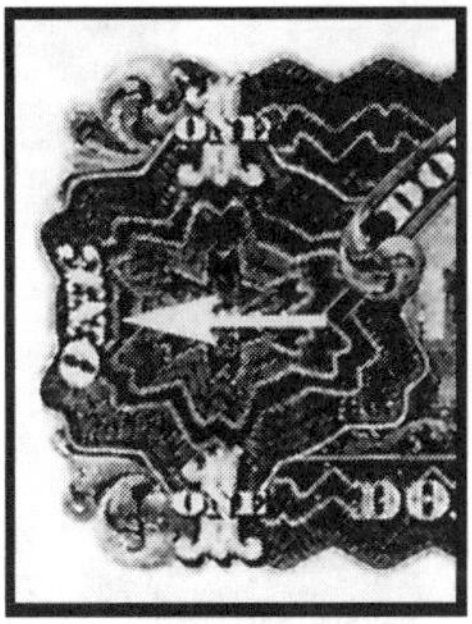

Inward "One" 1898

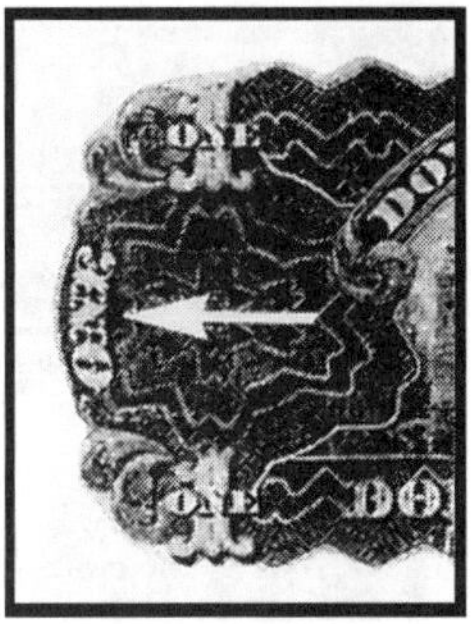

Outward "One" 1898

Denom.	Issue Date	Variety/Signature	Buying Price
$1	1897	Green face tint	300.00
$2	1897	Red-brown back	2,500.00
$2	1897	Dark brown back	200.00
$1	1898	Inward "One"	110.00
$1	1898	Outward "One"	75.00

1900 AND 1902 ISSUES

"4" on Top

"Four" on Top

Denom.	Issue Date	Variety/Signature	Buying Price
25-cent	1900	Courtney	3.00
25-cent	1900	Bouville	3.00
25-cent	1900	Saunders	3.00
$4	1900		675.00
$4	1902	"4" on Top	925.00
$4	1902	"Four" on Top	425.00

Note: The buying prices listed are for notes in **Very Good (VG)** condition.

1911 AND 1912 ISSUES

No Seal

Seal over Five

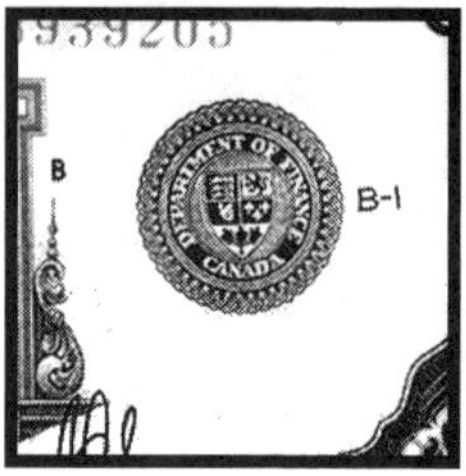

Seal Only

Denom.	Issue Date	Variety/Signature	Buying Price
$1	1911	Green Line or Black Line	45.00
$500	1911		15,000.00
$1,000	1911		12,000.00
$5	1912	No Seal	375.00
$5	1912	Seal over Five	375.00
$5	1912	Seal Only	350.00

1914 AND 1917 ISSUES

Denom.	Issue Date	Variety/Signature	Buying Price
$2	1914	No Seal	60.00
$2	1914	Seal over Two	125.00
$2	1914	Seal Only	100.00
$1	1917	No Seal	35.00
$1	1917	Seal over One	35.00
$1	1917	Black Seal	35.00

Note: The buying prices listed are for notes in **Very Good (VG)** condition.

1923 ISSUES

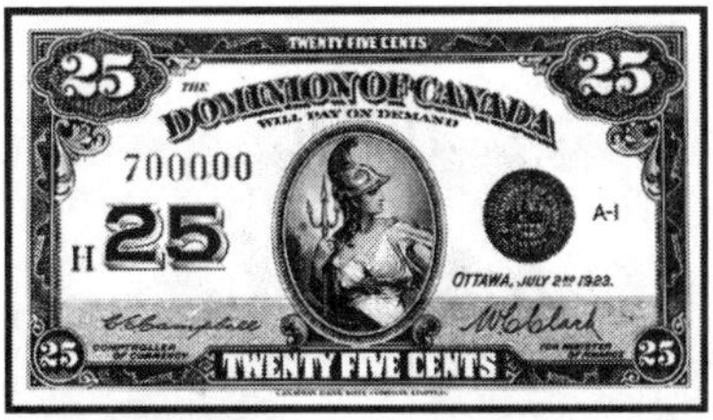

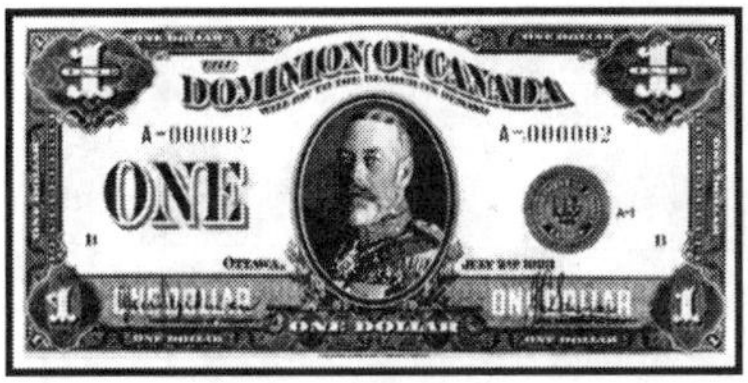

Denom.	Issue Date	Variety/Signature	Buying Price
25-cent	1923	Hyndman/Saunders	4.00
25-cent	1923	McCavour/Saunders	2.00
25-cent	1923	Campbell/Clark	2.00
$1	1923	Various Colour Seals	15.00
$1	1923	Purple Seal	75.00
$2	1923	Various Colour Seals	30.00
$2	1923	Green Seal	40.00
$2	1923	Bronze Seal	30.00

1924 AND 1925 ISSUES

Denom.	Issue Date	Variety/Signature	Buying Price
$5	1924	Queen Mary	2,000.00
$500	1925	George V	7,500.00
$1,000	1925	Queen Mary	8,000.00

Note: The buying prices listed are for notes in **Very Good (VG)** condition.

BANK OF CANADA

1935 ISSUES

Denom.	Variety	Buying Price
$1	English text	14.00
$1	French text	30.00
$2	English text	25.00
$2	French text	100.00
$5	English text	45.00
$5	French text	60.00
$10	English text	45.00
$10	French text	75.00
$20	English text	250.00
$20	French text	375.00
$25	English text	1,000.00
$25	French text	1,200.00
$50	English text	600.00
$50	French text	900.00
$100	English text	400.00
$100	French text	700.00
$500	English or French	8,500.00
$1,000	English or French	1,500.00

Note: The buying prices listed are for notes in **Very Good (VG)** condition.

1937 ISSUES

IMPORTANT

Bank notes with tears, missing corners, pinholes or folding creases are not considered to be very fine (VF). Notes in poor condition are not collectable.

	Very Fine Buying Prices By Signature		
Denom.	Osborne	Gordon	Coyne
$1	12.00	5.00	5.00
$2	20.00	11.00	11.00
$5	55.00	9.00	9.00
$10	30.00	11.00	11.00
$20	35.00	21.00	21.00
$50	200.00	55.00	55.00
$100	125.00	100.00	100.00
$1,000	1,100.00	NI	NI

Note: 1. NI - Not issued.
2. The buying prices listed are for notes in **Very Fine (VF)** condition.

1954 ISSUES

"DEVIL'S FACE" PORTRAIT

IMPORTANT

The buying prices listed below are for notes in very fine condition. The note must be clean, crisp, with no tears, creases, folds or marks of any kind or description folds.

THE DEVIL'S FACE NOTES

On the earliest notes of the 1954 issue, highlighted areas of the Queen's hair produced the illusion of a leering demonic face behind her ear. This was not the result of an error, nor was it, as some have asserted, the prank of an IRA sympathizer at the bank note company. It was merely the faithful reproduction of the original photograph. The portrait of the Queen with the devil's face outlined in her hair generated almost instant controversy.

ASTERISK NOTES

Asterisk notes are replacement notes, the first being spoiled in printing, cutting, etc., and replaced by an asterisk note. The asterisk is a small star-like symbol which appears before the prefix letters and serial number.

	Very Fine Buying Price by Signature			
	Coyne/Towers		Beattie/Coyne	
Denom.	Regular	Asterisk	Regular	Asterisk
$1	9.00	400.00	7.00	300.00
$2	20.00	500.00	8.00	400.00
$5	22.00	1,750.00	18.00	900.00
$10	15.00	700.00	10.00	400.00
$20	25.00	900.00	20.00	500.00
$50	50.00	NI	55.00	NI
$100	100.00	NI	110.00	NI
$1,000	1,200.00	NI	NI	NI

Note: 1. NI - Not Issued
2. The buying prices listed are for notes in **Very Fine (VF)** condition.

MODIFIED PORTRAIT

IMPORTANT

The buying prices listed below are for notes in uncirculated condition (new). The note must be clean, crisp, with no tears, creases, folds or marks of any kind or description.

MODIFIED PORTRAIT

The portrait was modified by darkening the highlights in the hair and thus removing the shading which had resulted in the devil's face. The modification of the face plates was made for most denominations in 1956, except for the $1,000 denomination, which was modified several years later.

Uncirculated Buying Price by Signature

Denom.	Beattie/Coyne Regular	Beattie/Coyne Asterisk	Beattie/Rasminsky Regular	Beattie/Rasminsky Asterisk	Bouey/Raminsky Regular	Bouey/Raminsky Asterisk	Lawson/Bouey Regular	Lawson/Bouey Asterisk
$1	4.00	50.00	3.00	5.00	3.00	20.00	3.00	25.00
$2	13.00	150.00	4.00	8.00	5.00	11.00	5.00	36.00
$5	20.00	170.00	10.00	80.00	10.00	60.00	NI	NI
$10	30.00	300.00	15.00	40.00	NI	NI	NI	NI
$20	35.00	400.00	25.00	350.00	NI	NI	NI	NI
$50	110.00	NI	80.00	NI	NI	NI	90.00	NI
$100	125.00	NI	110.00	NI	NI	NI	125.00	NI
$1,000	1,400.00	NI	1,100.00	NI	1,100.00	NI	1,100.00	NI

Note: **1.** NI - Not Issued
2. The above buying prices are for strictly uncirculated bank notes.

$1 CENTENNIAL 1967

For the centennial of Canada's Confederation a special $1 note was issued. The note has a single design and two types of serial numbers, regular serial numbers and a special number "1867 - 1967." The special series was available from the Bank of Canada as a collector's item, but examples were soon found in circulation. In addition, there was an asterisk note series for replacement notes.

Denom.	Issue Date	Variety	Uncirculated Buying Price
$1	1967	Commemorative Serial Number 1867-1967	1.05
$1	1967	Regular Serial Number	2.00
$1	1967	Asterisk Serial Number	20.00

1969 - 1975 ISSUE

This new series combined fine line engraving with subtle variations to make notes that are extremely difficult to counterfeit. The series features a new portrait of the Queen, as well as portraits of previous prime ministers of Canada.

IMPORTANT

The buying prices listed on the following page are for notes in uncirculated condition (new). The note must be clean, crisp, with no tears, creases, folds or marks of any kind or description.

1969-1975 ISSUES

ASTERISK AND "X" REPLACEMENT NOTES

Replacement of defective notes by asterisk notes was continued when the 1969-1975 issue was introduced. The highest denomination of the 1954 issue to be printed with asterisks was the $20; however, all denominations in the 1969-1975 issue, including the $50 and $100 notes, occur with asterisks in front of the two-letter prefix type.

When the triple-letter prefix notes were introduced in 1981, the use of the asterisk was discontinued. For triple-letter prefix notes, a replacement note was then designated by the use of an "X" for the third letter.

Asterisk Notes
BC-46aA

"X" Replacement Notes
BC-46A-i

	Uncirculated Buying Price by Signature									
	Beattie/Rasminsky		Bouey/Rasminsky		Lawson/Bouey			Crow/Bouey	
Denom.	Regular	Asterisk	Regular	Asterisk	Regular	Asterisk	X	Regular	X
$1	NI	NI	NI	NI	1.	5.	15.	1.	7.
$2	NI	NI	NI	NI	4.	20.	95.	4.	150.
$5	NI	NI	12.	60.	10.	65.	NI	NI	NI
$10	25.	50.	20.	90.	15.	100.	500.	15.	40.
$20	40.	125.	NI	NI	25.	100.	NI	NI	NI
$50	NI	NI	NI	NI	90.	400.	1,200.	60.	100.
$100	NI	NI	NI	NI	110.	600.	1,200.	110.	150.

Note: **1.** Thiessen/Crow signatures will be found on $10 regular notes. These are face value.
2. NI - Not Issued

1979 ISSUES

The series beginning in 1979 is a modification of the previous issue. The face designs are similar, as is the colouration. The serial numbers are moved to the back of the note at the bottom, where the name of the Bank of Canada previously appeared. The black serial numbers are machine readable.

IMPORTANT

The buying prices listed below are for notes in uncirculated condition (new). The note must be clean, crisp, with no tears, creases, folds or marks of any kind or description.

REPLACEMENT NOTES

There are no asterisk notes in this issue. The replacement notes are designated by the second digit in the serial number.
The digit 1 following the first digit 3 of the $5 notes designates a replacement note. In the $20 denomination the replacement notes can be distinguished by "510" for the CBN company and "516" for the BABN company.

$5 Replacement Note

$20 Replacement Note

	Uncirculated Buying Price by Signature					
	Lawson/Bouey		Crow/Bouey		Thiessen/Crow	
Denom.	Regular	Replace.	Regular	Replace.	Regular	Replace.
$5	10.00	250.00	20.00	400.00	NI	NI
$20	25.00	600.00	25.00	150.00	20.00	60.00

Note: Prices listed are buying prices for notes in new (uncirculated) condition.

1986 BIRD ISSUES

On March 14, 1986, the Bank of Canada introduced a new series of bank notes. The new designs were launched that year with the issue of the $2 and $5 notes. The $1 and $2 bank notes have since been replaced with $1 and $2 coins.

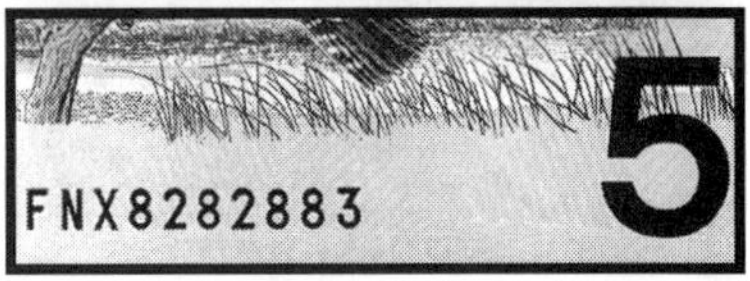

$5 Replacement Note

Denom.	Signature	Regular	Replacement
$2	Crow / Bouey	4.00	25.00
$5	Crow / Bouey	12.00	85.00

	Uncirculated Buying Price by Signature							
	Theissen/Crow		Bonin/Theissen		Knight/Thiessen		Knight/Dodge	
Denom.	Regular	Replace.	Regular	Replace.	Regular	Replace.	Regular	Replace.
$2	3.00	5.00	2.00	3.00	NI	NI	NI	NI
$5	5.00	15.00	5.00	75.00	5.00	60.00	5.00	40.00
$10	12.00	35.00	10.00	150.00	10.00	NI	NI	NI
$20	22.00	40.00	20.00	40.00	20.00	100.00	20.00	30.00
$50	60.00	90.00	50.00	NI	50.00	NI	50.00	100.00
$100	110.00	250.00	100.00	NI	100.00	NI	100.00	175.00
$1000	1,000.00	1,300.00	1,000.00	NI	NI	NI	NI	NI

Note: Prices listed are buying prices for notes in new (uncirculated) condition

2001 JOURNEY ISSUES

Without Security Device

With Security Device

Without Security Device

With Security Device

	Uncirculated Buying Price by Signature		
Denom.	**Knight/Thiessen**	**Knight/Dodge**	**Jenkins/Dodge**
$5 Without Security Device	NI	5.00	5.00
$5 With Security Device	NI	NI	5.00
$10 Without Security Device	10.00	10.00	10.00
$10 With Security Device	NI	NI	10.00
$20 With Security Device	NI	NI	20.00
$50 With Security Device	NI	NI	50.00
$100 With Security Device	NI	NI	100.00

Note: 1. Prices listed are buying prices for notes in new (uncirculated) condition.
2. No identifiable replacement notes have been printed for this issue.

NEWFOUNDLAND
PUBLIC WORKS CASH NOTES

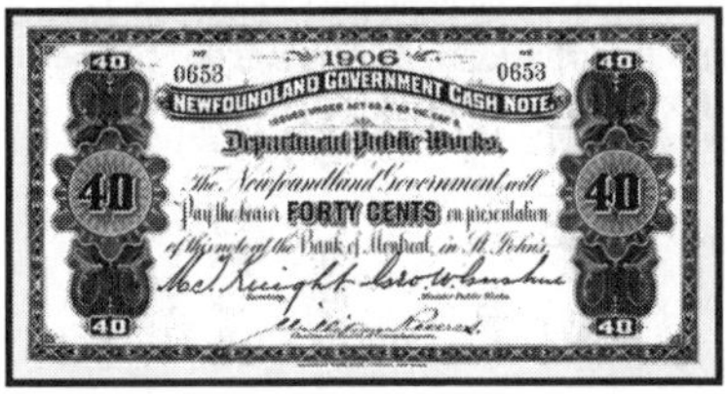

1901-1909

Denom.	Buying Price
40 cents	150.00
50 cents	175.00
80 cents	200.00
$1	150.00
$5	750.00

1910-1911

Denom.	Buying Price
25 cents	75.00
50 cents	75.00
$1	100.00
$2	650.00
$5	800.00

GOVERNMENT NOTES

Denom.	Buying Price
$1	75.00
$2	150.00

PRINCE EDWARD ISLAND

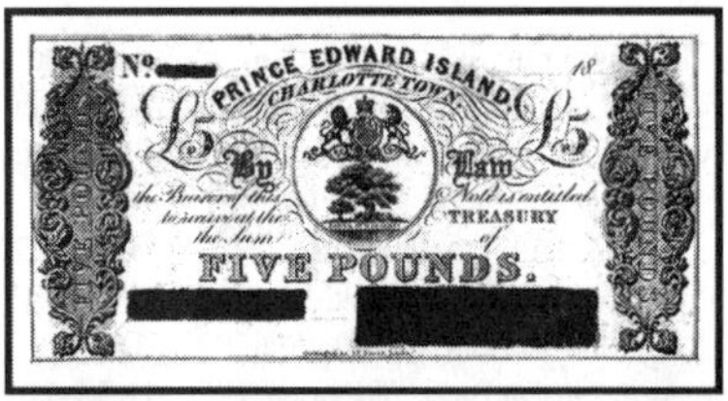

Denom.	Buying Price
1848-1870 5s	600.00
1848-1870 10s	600.00
1848-1870 £1	600.00
1848-1870 £2	600.00
1848-1870 £5	600.00
1872 $10	1,500.00
1872 $20	1,500.00

NOVA SCOTIA

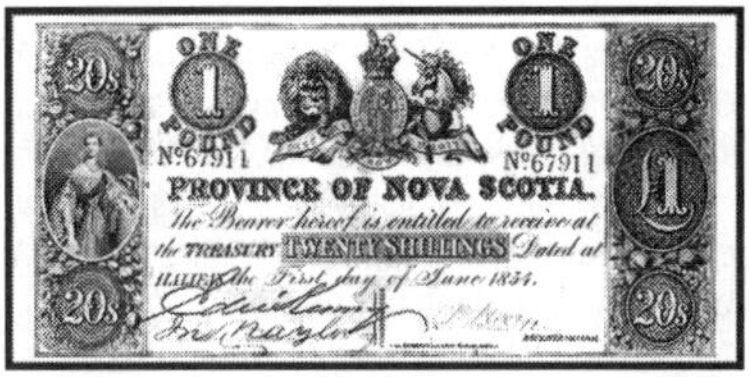

Denom.	Buying Price
1848-1854 £1	900.00
1861 $5	1,000.00

Note: Prices given are for notes in VG or better condition.

CANADIAN NOTE-ISSUING BANKS

The following list of Canadian banks issued various denominational bank noted between 1813 and 1943. All these notes command a premium over face value. If you have any of the notes do not take them to your Bank, check with your local numismatic dealer for their current buying price.

The Bank of Acadia, Liverpool, N.S., 1872-1873
The Accommodation Bank, Kingston, U.C., 1836-1837
The Agricultural Bank, Montreal, L.C., 1837
The Agricultural Bank, Toronto, U.C., 1834-1837
Arman's Bank, Montreal, L.C., 1837
Barclay's Bank (Canada), Montreal, Que., 1929-1956
La Banque du Boucherville, Boucherville, L.C., 1830's
The Bank of Brantford, Brantford, C.W., 1857-1860's
The British Canadian Bank, Toronto, Ont., 1883-1884
The Bank of British Columbia, Victoria, B.C., 1862-1901
The Bank of British North America, 1836-1918
Canada Bank, Montreal, L.C., 1792
The Canada Bank, Toronto, C.W., 1855
The Bank of Canada, Montreal, L.C., 1813-1831
The Canadian Bank of Commerce, Toronto, Ont., 1867-1961
Banque Canadienne, St. Hyacinthe, L.C., 1836-1838
Banque Canadienne Nationale, Montreal, Que., 1924-1979
The Central Bank of Canada, Toronto, Ont., 1883-1887
Central Bank of New Brunswick, Fredericton, N.B., 1834-1866
Charlotte County Bank, St. Andrew's, N.B., 1825-1865
Bank of Charlottetown, Charlottetown, P.E.I., 1852
The City Bank, Montreal, L.C., 1833-1876
City Bank, Saint John, N.B., 1836-1839
The Bank of Clifton, C.W., 1859-1863
The Colonial Bank of Canada, Toronto, C.W., 1856-1863
The Colonial Bank of Chatham, Chatham, U.C., 1837-1839
Commerical Bank, Brockville, U.C., 1837
Commercial Bank, Kingston, U.C., 1837
The Commercial Bank of Canada, Kingston, C.W., 1856-1868
The Commercial Bank of Fort Erie, Fort Erie, U.C., 1836-1839
The Commercial Bank of Lake Ontario, Niagara Falls, U.C., 1837
The Commercial Bank of Manitoba, Winnipeg, Man., 1885-1893
The Commerical Bank of the Midland District, Kingston, U.C., 1831-1856
Commerical Bank of Montreal, Montreal, L.C., 1835-1837
Commercial Bank of New Brunswick, Saint John, N.B., 1834-1868
The Commercial Bank of Newfoundland, St. John's, Nfld., 1857-1894
Commercial Bank of Windsor, Windsor, N.S., 1864-1902
Commerical Branch Bank of Canada, Collingwood, C.W., 1861-1879
The Consolidated Bank of Canada, Montreal, Que., 1876-1879
The Bank of the County of Elgin, St. Thomas, C.W., 1857-1862
The Crown Bank of Canada, Toronto, Ont., 1904-1908
The Dominion Bank, Toronto, Ont., 1869-1955
Eastern Bank of Canada, Saint John, N.B., 1928-1934
The Eastern Townships Bank, Sherbrooke, C.E., 1855-1912
The Exchange Bank, Quebec, L.C., 1840's
The Exchange Bank of Canada, Montreal, Que., 1871-1883
The Exchange Bank of Canada, Windsor, Ont., 1860's
The Exchange Bank of Toronto, C.W., 1855
The Exchange Bank of Yarmouth, Yarmouth, N.S., 1867-1903
The Exchange Bank Company of Chippewa, Chippewa, U.C., 1837
The Farmer's Bank, Toronto, U.C., 1840's

The Farmers Bank of Canada, Toronto, Ont., 1906-1910
The Farmer's Bank of Malden, Maiden, U.C., 1840's
The Farmer's Joint Stock Banking Co., Toronto, U.C., 1835-1849
The Farmers J.S. Banking Co., Toronto, U.C., 1830's
The Farmers Bank of Rustico, Rustico, P.E.I., 1862-1892
The Farmers Bank of St. John's, St. John's, L.C., 1837-1838
The Federal Bank of Canada, Toronto, Ont., 1874-1888
The Bank of Fredericton, Fredericton, N.B., 1836-1839
The Free Holders Bank of the Midland District, Bath, U.C., 1837
Goderich Bank, Goderich, U.C., 1834
The Gore Bank, Hamilton, U.C., 1835-1870
The Gore Bank of Hamilton, Hamilton, U.C., c.1837
The Grenville County Bank, Prescott, C.W., 1856
The Halifax Banking Company, Halifax, N.S., 1825-1903
The Hamtilon Bank, Hamilton, L.C., 1835
The Bank of Hamilton, Hamilton, Ont., 1872-1923
Hart's Bank, Three Rivers, L.C., 1835-1847
Henry's Bank, La Prairie and Montreal, L.C., 1837
Banque d'Hochelaga, Montreal, Que., 1873-1925
The Home Bank of Canada, Toronto, Ont., 1903-1923
The Bank of Hull, Hull, L.C., 1837
The Imperial Bank of Canada, Toronto, Ont., 1873-1961
The International Bank of Canada, Toronto, U.C., 1858-1859
Banque Internationale du Canada, Montreal, Que., 1911-1913
La Banque Jacques Cartier, Montreal, C.E., 1861-1900
The Kingston Bank, Kingston, L.C., 1837
The Bank of Liverpool, Liverpool, N.S., 1871-1879
The Bank of London in Canada, London, Ont., 1883-1888
Lower Canada Bank, Montreal, L.C., 1837
The Bank of Lower Canada, Quebec, L.C., late 1830's MacDonald & Co., Victoria, B.C., 1859-1866
The Maritime Bank of the Dominon of Canada, Saint John, N.B., 1872-1887
The Mechanics Bank, Montreal, L.C., 1837
The Mechanics Bank, Montreal, C.E., 1865-1879
The Mechanics Bank of Saint John's, Saint John's, L.C., 1837
The Mercantile Banking Corporation, Halifax, N.S., 1878
The Merchants Bank, Montreal, C.E., 1864-1868
The Merchants Bank, Toronto, U.C., 1837
The Merchants Bank of Canada, Montreal, Que., 1868-1923
The Merchants Bank of Halifax, Halifax, N.S., 1864-1901
The Merchants Bank of Prince Edward Island, Charlottetown, P.E.I., 1871-1906
The Merchants Exchange Bank, Goderich, C.W., 1853
The Metropolitan Bank, Montreal, Que., 1871-1876
The Metropolitan Bank, Toronto, 1902-1914
The Molsons Bank, Montreal, C.E., 1837-1925
Montreal Bank, Montreal, L.C., 1817-1822
The Montreal Bank, Montreal, C.W., 1840's-1950's
The Bank of Montreal, Montreal, L.C., 1822 to date
La Banque Nationale, Montreal, C.E., 1860-1925
The Bank of New Brunswick, Saint John, N.B., 1820-1913
The Newcastle Banking Co., Amherst, U.C., 1836
The Newcastle District Loan Company, Peterborough, U.C., 1836
The Newcastle District Bank, St. Catharines, C.W., 1853-1875
The Niagara Suspension Bridge Bank, Queenston, U.C., 1836-1841
The Northern Bank, Winnpeg, Man., 1905-1908
The Northern Crown Bank, Winnipeg, Man., 1908-1918
The Bank of Nova Scotia, Halifax, N.S., 1832 to date

The Ontario Bank, Bowmanville, C.W., 1857-1906
The Bank of Ottawa, Montreal, L.C., 1837
The Bank of Ottawa, Ont., 1874-1919
The Bank of the People, Toronto, U.C., 1835-1841
La Banque du Peuple, Montreal, L.C., 1835-1895
The People's Bank of Halifax, Halifax, N.S., 1864-1905
The People's Bank of New Brunswick, Fredericton, N.B., 1864-1907
The Phenix Bank, Phillipsburg, L.C., 1837-1841
The Pictou Bank, Pictou, N.S., 1873-1887
The Bank of Prince Edward Island, Charlottetonwn, P.E.I., 1856-1881
The Provincial Bank, London, Ont., 1884
The Provincial Bank of Canada, Stanstead, Ont., 1856-1863
La Banque Provinciale du Canada, Montreal, Que., 1900-1979
The Quebec Bank, Quebec, L.C., 1818-1917
Bank of Quebec Lower Canada, Quebec, L.C., 1841
The Royal Bank of Canada, Montreal, Que., 1901 to date
The Royal Canadian Bank, Toronto, C.W., 1864-1876
The Saint Francis Bank, Stanstead, C.E., 1855
La Banque de St. Hyacinthe St. Hyacinthe, Que., 1873-1908
La Banque de St. Jean, St. Jean, Que., 1873-1908
Banque St. Jean Baptiste, Montreal, Que., 1875
The St. Lawrence Bank, Toronto, Ont., 1872-1876
The St. Lawrence Bank & Lumber Co., Malbaie, L.C., 1837
The St. Stephen's Bank, St. Stephen, N.B., 1836-1910
The Bank of Saskatchewan, Moose Jaw, Sask., 1913
The Sovereign Bank of Canada, Montreal, Que., 1901-1908
The Stadacona Bank, Quebec City, Que., 1872-1879
The Standard Bank of Canada, Toronto,Ont., 1876-1928
The Sterling Bank of Canada, Toronto, Ont., 1905-1924
The Summerside Bank, Summerside, P.E.I., 1866-1901
Tattersall Bank, Montreal, L.C., 183-
The Bank of Toronto, Toronto, Ont., 1855-1954
The Traders Bank of Canada, Toronto, Ont., 1885-1912
The Union Bank, Montreal, L.C., 1838-c.1840
The Union Bank of Canada, Quebec City, Que., 1886-1925
THe Union Bank of Halifax, Halifax, N.S., 1856-1910
The Union Bank of Lower Canada, Quebec, C.E., 1865-1886
The Union Bank of Montreal, Montreal, L.C., c.1840
Union Bank of Newfoundland, St. John's, Nfld., 1854-1894
The Union Bank of Prince Edward Island, Charlottetown, P.E.I., 1860-1893
United Empire Bank of Canada, Toronto,Ont., 1906-1911
Bank of Upper Canada, Kingston, U.C., 1819-1822
Bank of Upper Canada, York, U.C., 1821-1866
The Bank of Vancouver, Vancouver, B.C., 1910-1914
The Bank of Victoria, Victoria, U.C., 1836
La Banque Ville Marie, Montreal, Que., 1872-1899
The Bank of Western Canada, Clifton, C.W., 1859-1863
The Western Bank of Canada, Oshawa, Ont., 1882-1909
The Westmoreland Bank of New Brunswick, N.B., 1854-1867
The Weyburn Security Bank, Weyburn, Sask., 1910-1931
The Bank of Yarmouth, Yarmouth, N.S., 1859-1905
The Zimmerman Bank, Elgin., C.W., 1854-1859

CANADIAN COLONIAL TOKENS

Canada has produced a great number of tokens of various kinds over the years. Tokens were used as a form of currency prior to the institution of the decimal currency system in 1858 (Colonial issues are not all tokens, some being regal coins). After Confederation, other kinds of tokens appeared, such as those for services, transportation and advertising purposes.
The prices in this section are for tokens in VG (very good) or F (fine) condition. Higher prices will be paid for rare issues or for tokens in VF (very fine) or better condition.

NEWFOUNDLAND TOKENS

Date and Description	Buying Price
Rutherford - St. John's	4.00
Rutherford - Harbour Grace	4.00
McAuslane	2,250.00

Date and Description	Buying Price
1858 Sailing Ship	175.00
1860 Fishery Rights	22.00

PRINCE EDWARD ISLAND TOKENS

Date and Description	Buying Price
Holey Dollar Ring*	1,750.00
Holey Dollar Plug*	1,750.00
McCausland Penny	1,300.00
McCarthy Penny	1,750.00
Sheaf of Wheat	400.00
Speed The Plough	3.00

Note: * Forgeries exist and are worth considerably less.

PRINCE EDWARD ISLAND TOKENS

Date and Description	Buying Price
Fisheries & Agriculture	3.00
Self Government 1855 Prince Edward's	3.00
Self Government 1855 Prince Edward	3.00
Self Government 1857	3.00

Date and Description	Buying Price
Fisheries & Agriculture	3.00
Ships Colonies 1815 One Penny	10.00
Ships Colonies 1815 Publick Accommodation	10.00
Ships Colonies	3.50

Note: Tokens must be **VG (very good)** or better condition, with no discolouration or damage.

NOVA SCOTIA
SEMI-REGAL TOKENS

Date and Description	Buying Price
1823 Halfpenny	1.75
1823 Penny	3.00
1824 Halfpenny	1.75
1824 Penny	3.00
1832 Halfpenny	1.75
1832 Penny	3.00
1840 Halfpenny	1.75
1840 Penny	3.00
1843 Halfpenny	3.00
1843 Penny	6.00
1856 Halfpenny	3.00
1856 Penny	3.00

NOVA SCOTIA TOKENS

Date and Description	Buying Price
Broke - Halifax	4.00
Convenience of Trade	13.00
Carritt & Alport	6.00
Hosterman & Etter	6.00

Date and Description	Buying Price
Hosterman & Etter 1815	7.00
Starr & Shannon	3.00
Commercial Change	4.00
Miles W. White	4.00

NOVA SCOTIA TOKENS

Date and Description	Buying Price
John Alexr Barry	4.00
Halifax Nova Scotia	10.00
W. A. & S. Black's	10.00
J. Brown	4.00
W. L. White's	18.50
Trade & Navigation 1812	4.00
Trade & Navigation 1813	4.00
Pure Copper Preferable	3.00
Success to Navigation	3.00
N.S & N.B. Success	18.50

NEW BRUNSWICK TOKENS

Date and Description	Buying Price
1843 Halfpenny	1.50
1843 Penny	2.50
1854 Halfpenny	1.50
1854 Penny	2.50

Date and Description	Buying Price
McDermott	500.00
St. John	6.00
St. John's	5,000.00

LOWER CANADA TOKENS

Date and Description	Buying Price
Magdalen Island	25.00
Bank Token	3.00
Banque du Peuple, Maple Leaf	4.00
Banque du Peuple, Wreath	1.75

Date and Description	Buying Price
Pro Bono Publico	2,250.00
Bank Token Halfpenny	1.75
Bank Token Penny	3.00
Bank of Montreal, Sideview Halfpenny	375.00
Bank of Montreal, Sideview Penny	575.00

LOWER CANADA TOKENS

Date and Description	Buying Price
Montreal Half Penny	3.00
Canada Half Penny	3.00
For Public Accommodation	4.00
T.S. Brown & Co.	3.00
Ths & Wm Molson	235.00

Date and Description	Buying Price
Francis Mullins & Son	5.00
R.W. Owen	5,000.00
J. Shaw & Co.	4.00
J. Roy	22.50
Agriculture & Commerce	1.75

LOWER CANADA TOKENS

Date and Description	Buying Price
Halfpenny Token 1812, Small Wreath	3.00
Halfpenny Token 1812, Large Wreath	3.00
Penny Token 1812	4.00
Victoria Nobis Est	4.00
R H Half Penny	4.00

Date and Description	Buying Price
To Facilitate Trade	
Military Bust 1825	4.00
Civilian Bust 1825	800.00
Spread Eagle	3.00
Halfpenny Token	5.00

LOWER CANADA TOKENS

Date and Description	Buying Price
Seated Justice	3.00
Bust/Ships Colonies	4.00

Date and Description	Buying Price
Commercial Change	3.00
Bust and Harp	6.00

WELLINGTON TOKENS

Date and Description	Buying Price
Field Marshal Wellington	3.00
Marquis Wellington	4.00

Date and Description	Buying Price
The Illustrious Wellington	3.00
Battle Token	3.00

Date and Description	Buying Price
Copper Company	500.00
Lesslie Halfpenny	5.00
Lesslie Twopenny	75.00
No Labour No Bread	3.00
Sir Isaac Brock	3.00

Date and Description	Buying Price
Success To Commerce	3.00
Upper & Lower Canada	22.50
Commercial Change 1815	22.50
Commerical Change 1820	3.00

UPPER CANADA TOKENS

Date and Description	Buying Price
Commercial Change 1821	
Cask Marked Upper Canada	22.50
Cask Marked Jamaica	285.00
Province of Upper Canada	12.00

Date and Description	Buying Price
To Facilitate Trade	
1823	3.00
1833	1.75
Commercial Change 1833	3.00

PROVINCE OF CANADA TOKENS

PROVINCE OF CANADA TOKENS

Date and Description	Buying Price
Bank of Montreal	
1842, 1844 Halfpenny	1.75
1845 Halfpenny	1,500.00
1837 Penny	60.00
1842 Penny	4.00

Date and Description	Buying Price
Quebec Bank, 1852 Halfpenny	1.75
Penny	3.00
Bank of Upper Canada 1850-1857	
Halfpenny	1.75
Penny	3.00

ANONYMOUS AND MISCELLANEOUS TOKENS

Date and Description	Buying Price
For General Accommodation	3.00
Success to Trade	15.00

Date and Description	Buying Price
Pure Copper Preferable	3.00
North American	18.50

BRITISH COLUMBIA TOKENS

Date and Description	Buying Price
1862 Pattern Gold $10	50,000.00
1862 Pattern Gold $20	50,000.00

NORTH WEST COMPANY

Date and Description	Buying Price
1820 North West Company Token	1,000.00

HUDSON'S BAY COMPANY

Date and Description	Buying Price
Hudson's Bay Company Tokens Set of four (1, ½, ¼, 1/8)	500.00

TRANSPORTATION TOKENS

Date and Description	Buying Price
Bridge Tokens, each	125.00
Montreal & Lachine Railroad	200.00
Montreal & Lachine Railroad Restrike Dated 1947	25.00

CANADIAN MEDALS

WAR MEDALS 1812 TO 1885

Army Gold Cross

Naval General Service Medal

Army Gold Medal

Canadian General Service Medal

Army General Service Medal

Egyptian Medal

Date and Description	Buying Price
Army Gold Cross	15,750.00
Army Gold Medal	6,000.00
Army General Service Medal 1812-1814	
Fort Detroit Bar	2,000.00
Chateauguay Bar	2,000.00
Chrysler's Farm Bar	2,000.00
Naval General Service Medal 1812-1814	200.00

Date and Description	Buying Price
Canadian General Service Medal	
Fenian Raid Bar 1866	150.00
Fenian Raid Bar 1870	150.00
Red River Bar 1870	550.00
Egyptian Medal*	
The Nile Bar	550.00
Kirbekan Bar	550.00

*Awarded to Canadian Boatmen

WAR MEDALS 1885 TO 1914

Khedive's Bronze Star

1914 Star

North West Canada Medal

1914-1915 Star

South Africa Medal

British War Medal

Date and Description	Buying Price
Khedive's Bronze Star	30.00
North West Canada Medal 1885	200.00
Saskatchewan Bar	250.00
Queen's South Africa	
1899-1900 on reverse	2,500.00
Dates removed	30.00
King's South Africa	30.00

Date and Description	Buying Price
1914 Star*	900.00
1914-1915 Star	7.50
British War Medal	11.00
Groups**	
Star, British War Medal (2)	30.00
Star, Allied Victory Medal British War Medal (3)	35.00

*Canadian Star awarded only to 2nd. Field Hospital.
**Groups to Canadian Veterans, named to same person

WAR MEDALS 1914 TO 1945

Allied Victory Medal

Canadian Defence Medal

Merchantile Marine War Medal

Canadian WW II 1939-1945 War Medal

Canadian Volunteer Service Medal

Atlantic
Air Crew Europe
Africa
France and Germany
Italy
Pacific
Burma

Date and Description	Buying Price
Allied Victory Medal	7.50
Merchantile Marine War Medal	11.00
Canadian Volunteer Service Medal	11.00
Defence Medal	11.00
1939-1945 War Medal	11.00

Date and Description	Buying Price
1939-1945 Star	6.00
Atlantic Star	17.50
Air Crew Europe	55.00
Africa Star	6.00
France and Germany Star	6.00
Italy Star	6.00
Pacific Star	11.00
Burma Star	11.00

Note: The Canadian Volunteer Service Medal, the Canadian Defence Medal and the World War II Medal are issued in silver. Britain and other Commonwealth countries issued cupro-nickel medals.

WAR MEDALS 1951 TO 1973

Canadian Korean Medal

United Nations Korea Medal

United Nations Emergency Medal

Date and Description	Buying Price
Canadian Korean War Medal, English	30.00
Canadian Korean War Medal, French	40.00
United Nations Korea Medal	17.50
United Nations Emergency Medal	17.50
United Nations Medal 1960 to present	17.50
International Commission Medal 1967	17.50
International Commission Medal 1973	17.50

COMMEMORATIVE MEDALS

1911 Coronation Medal

1935 Silver Jubilee Medal

1937 Coronation Medal

Date and Description	Buying Price
King George V	
Coronation Medal - 1911	22.00
Silver Jubilee Medal - 1935	17.50
King George VI	
Coronation Medal - 1937	17.50

COMMEMORATIVE MEDALS

1953
Coronation
Medal

1977
Silver
Jubilee
Medal

1967
Canadian
Centennial
Medal

MEDALS FOR VALOUR AND SERVICE

Victoria
Cross

Distinguished
Service
Order

Order of
St. Michael
and
St. George

Date and Description	Buying Price
Queen Elizabeth II	
Coronation Medal - 1953	17.50
Silver Jubilee Medal - 1977	40.00
Canadian Centennial Medal - 1967	30.00

Date and Description	Buying Price
Victoria Cross	40,000.00
Awarded to a Canadian	65,000.00
Distinguished Service Order	225.00
Order of St. Michael and St. George	225.00

Distinguished Service Cross

Air Force Medal

Distinguished Flying Cross

Military Medal

Air Force Cross

British Empire Medal

Date and Description	Buying Price
Distinguished Service Cross	275.00
Distinguished Flying Cross	375.00
Air Force Cross	450.00

Date and Description	Buying Price
Air Force Medal	150.00
Military Medal	200.00
British Empire Medal	55.00

COINS OF THE UNITED STATES

MINT MARKS

The United States decimal coinage is identified by the following mint marks:

C	-Charlotte, North Carolina
CC	-Carson City, Nevada
D	-Dahlonega, Georgia (gold coins only)
D	-Denver, Colorado (1906 to date)
O	-New Orleans, Louisiana
S	-San Francisco, California
P	-Philadelphia, Pennsylvania

HALF CENTS

Liberty Cap

Date and Mint Mark	Buying Price
1793 Head Facing Left	900.00
1794	200.00
1795	110.00
1796	4,000.00
1797	165.00

Draped Bust

Date and Mint Mark	Buying Price
1800	25.00
1802	400.00
1803-1808	25.00

Classic Head

Date and Mint Mark	Buying Price
1809-1810	10.00
1811	100.00
1825 to 1830	17.00
1831	1,000.00
1832 to 1835	12.50

Coronet Head

Date and Mint Mark	Buying Price
1849 to 1851	15.00
1852	350.00
1853 to 1856	25.00
1857	30.00

IMPORTANT NOTICE:
Buying prices are for coins in VG condition.

LARGE CENTS

Flowing Hair

Date and Mint Mark	Buying Price
1793 Chain Reverse	2,000.00
1793 Wreath Reverse	875.00

Liberty Cap

Date and Mint Mark	Buying Price
1793	1,500.00
1794	100.00
1795	75.00
1796	100.00

Draped Bust

Date and Mint Mark	Buying Price
1796	100.00
1797	45.00
1798	25.00
1799	800.00
1800 to 1803	25.00
1804	250.00
1805 to 1807	20.00

Classic Head

Date and Mint Mark	Buying Price
1808	50.00
1809	100.00
1810	25.00
1811	45.00
1812 to 1814	25.00

Coronet Head

Date and Mint Mark	Buying Price
1816 to 1820	9.00
1821	20.00
1822	9.00
1823	30.00
1824 to 1838	7.00
1839 to 1856	7.00
1857	40.00

SMALL CENTS

Flying Eagle

Date and Mint Mark	Buying Price
1856	3,000.00
1857 to 1858	7.00

Indian Head

Date and Mint Mark	Buying Price
1859	4.00
1860 to 1865	3.00
1866 to 1868	14.00
1869 to 1872	25.00
1873 to 1876	7.00
1877	300.00
1878	9.00
1879 to 1886	1.00
1887 to 1908	.25
1908S	20.00
1909	.75
1909S	150.00

Lincoln Head Wheat Ears

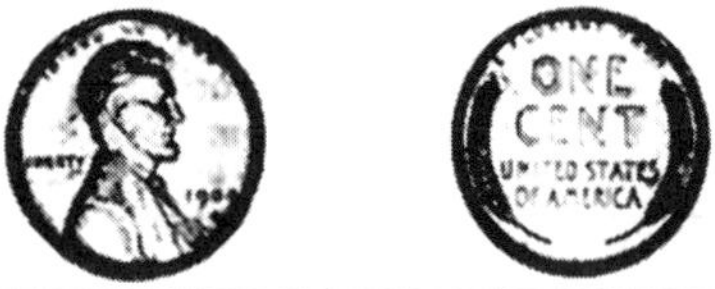

Date and Mint Mark	Buying Price
1909	.50
1909VDB	1.00
1909S	20.00
1909S VDB	200.00
1910 to 1914	.10
1914D	60.00
1915D to 1931D	.05
1931S	22.00
1932 to 1958	.01
1955 Double Die	100.00

Lincoln Head Memorial

Date and Mint Mark	Buying Price
1959 to 2006	.01

TWO CENTS

Date and Mint Mark	Buying Price
1864 to 1871	4.00
1872	100.00
1873 Proofs only	475.00

THREE CENTS

Silver

Date and Mint Mark	Buying Price
1851 to 1862	10.00
1863 to 1872	125.00
1873 Proofs only	200.00

Nickel

Date and Mint Mark	Buying Price
1865 to 1874	4.00
1875 to 1876	7.00
1877 to 1878 Proofs only	200.00
1879 to 1880	18.00
1881	4.00
1882	35.00
1883	55.00
1884 to 1887	120.00
1888	16.00
1889	30.00

HALF DIMES

Flowing Hair

Date and Mint Mark	Buying Price
1794	375.00
1795	300.00

Draped Bust

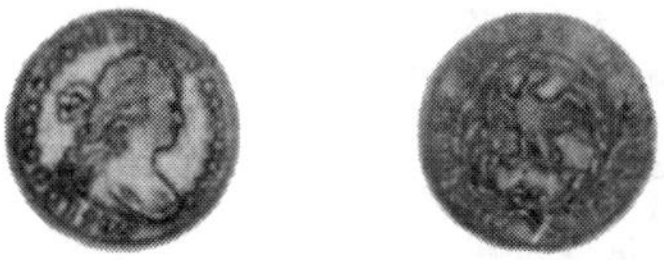

Date and Mint Mark	Buying Price
1796 to 1797	400.00
1800 to 1801	225.00
1802	6,000.00
1803 to 1805	275.00

Capped Bust

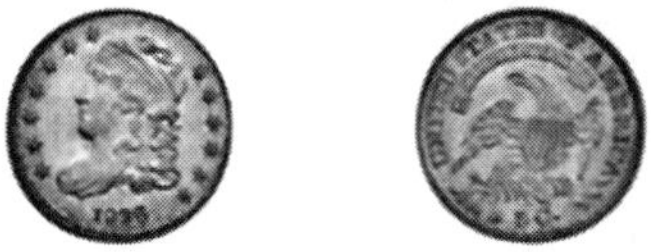

Date and Mint Mark	Buying Price
1829 to 1837	9.00

Liberty Seated

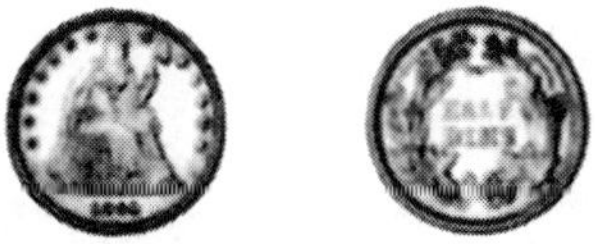

Date and Mint Mark	Buying Price
1837 Large Date	10.00
1837 Small Date	10.00
1838 to 1845	4.00
1838 O	30.00

Date and Mint Mark	Buying Price
1846	140.00
1847 to 1862	4.00
1863	65.00
1863S	11.00
1864	120.00
1864S	20.00
1865	120.00
1865S	10.00
1866	120.00
1866S	10.00
1867	160.00
1867S to 1873S	5.00

FIVE CENTS NICKEL

Shield

Date and Mint Mark	Buying Price
1866 to 1870	6.00
1871	20.00
1872 to 1876	9.00
1877 and 1878 Proofs only	265.00
1879 to 1881	100.00
1882 to 1883	5.00

Liberty Head

Date and Mint Mark	Buying Price
1883 to 1884	8.00
1885	160.00
1886	75.00
1887 to 1896	2.00
1897 to 1912D	.25
1912S	55.00

Indian Head

Date and Mint Mark	Buying Price
1913 and 1913D	2.00
1913S	25.00
1914D	35.00
1914S	15..
1914 to 1918	1.00
1918D 8/7	550.00
1919 to 1938	.15

Jefferson Head

Date and Mint Mark	Buying Price
1938 to 2003	.05

DIMES

Draped Bust

Date and Mint Mark	Buying Price
1796 to 1797	650.00
1798 to 1807	150.00

Capped Bust

Date and Mint Mark	Buying Price
1809 to 1811	50.00
1814 to 1821	8.00
1822	200.00
1823 to 1837	8.00

Liberty Seated

Date and Mint Mark	Buying Price
1837O and 1838O No stars	12.00
1838 to 1840O Stars	5.00
1841 to 1843	5.00
1843O	20.00
1844	100.00
1845 to 1845O	5.00
1846	50.00
1847 to 1856	4.00
1856S	65.00
1857 to 1860	4.00
1858S	40.00
1859S	50.00
1860O	150.00
1861 to 1862	4.00
1863	100.00
1863S	10.00
1864	50.00
1864S	10.00
1865	100.00
1865S	10.00
1866	125.00
1866S	15.00
1867	150.00
1867S	15.00
1868 to 1874	5.00
1871CC	800.00
1872CC	300.00
1873CC Arrows	600.00
1874CC Arrows	1,000.00
1875 to 1878	4.00
1878CC	35.00
1879 to 1881	60.00
1882 to 1885	4.00
1885S	150.00
1886 to 1891	3.50

Barber

Date and Mint Mark	Buying Price
1892 to 1895	4.00
1895O	150.00
1896O	50.00
1897 to 1916	.70

Mercury Head

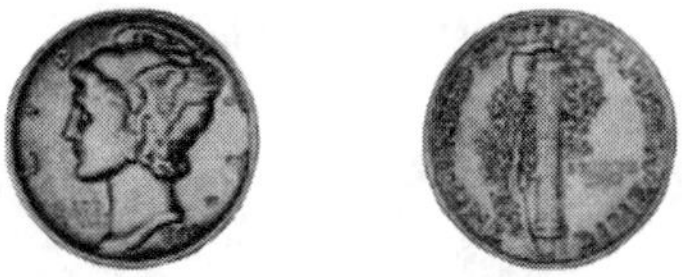

Date and Mint Mark	Buying Price
1916	.70
1916D	525.00
1917 to 1945	.70
1921	22.00
1921D	40.00

Roosevelt - Silver

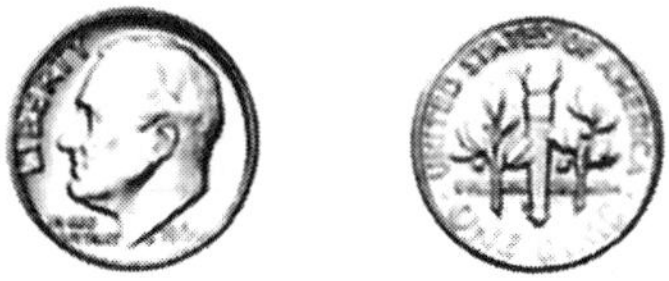

Date and Mint Mark	Buying Price
1946 to 1964	.70

Roosevelt - Clad

Date and Mint Mark	Buying Price
1965 to 2006	.40

TWENTY CENTS

Date and Mint Mark	Buying Price
1875 to 1876	30.00
1877 to 1878 Proofs only	500.00

QUARTER DOLLAR

Draped Bust

Date and Mint Mark	Buying Price
1796	3,500.00
1804	1,150.00
1805 to 1807	85.00

Capped Bust

Date and Mint Mark	Buying Price
1815 to 1822	40.00
1823/2	5,000.00
1824 to 1828	25.00
1831 to 1838 Reduced Size	30.00

Liberty Seated

Date and Mint Mark	Buying Price
1838 to 1841	7.00
1842 Large Date	35.00
1842 Small Date	150.00
1842O Small Date	10.00
1843 to 1849	7.00
1849O	175.00
1850 to 1851	8.00
1851O	90.00
1852	18.00
1852O	85.00
1853 to 1865	6.00
1862S to 1865S	15.00
1864S	125.00
1866 to 1867S	90.00
1868 to 1870	25.00
1870CC and 1871CC	700.00
1871 to 1878CC	7.00
1871S	100.00
1872CC	300.00
1872S	275.00
1878S to 1888	40.00
1888S	5.00
1889 and 1890	90.00
1891O	65.00
1891 and 1891S	5.00

Barber

Date and Mint Mark	Buying Price
1892 to 1896	2.00
1896S	300.00
1897 to 1901	2.00
1901S	3,000.00
1902 to 1913	2.00
1913S	800.00
1914 to 1916D	2.00

Standing Liberty

Date and Mint Mark	Buying Price
1916	2,000.00
1917 to 1924	10.00
1923S	125.00
1925 to 1930	2.00

Washington - Silver

Date and Mint Mark	Buying Price
1932 to 1964	1.70
1927S	10.00
1932D	.50
1932S	.50
1933 to 1964	1.70

Washington - Clad

Date and Mint Mark	Buying Price
1965 to 1975	1.00

200th Bi-Centennial

Date and Mint Mark	Buying Price
1976	.25

STATE QUARTERS

Delaware

Pennsylvania

Maryland

South Carolina

New Jersey

Georgia

New Hampshire

Virginia

Connecticut

Massachusetts

New York

North Carolina

Date and Mint Mark	Description	Buying Price
1999P	Delaware, MS	.25
1999D	Delaware, MS	.25
1999S	Delaware, PR	2.00
1999P	Pennsylvania, MS	.25
1999D	Pennsylvania, MS	.25
1999S	Pennsylvania, PR	2.00
1999P	New Jersey, MS	.25
1999D	New Jersey, MS	.25
1999S	New Jersey, PR	2.00
1999P	Georgia, MS	.25
1999D	Georgia, MS	.25
1999S	Georgia, PR	2.00
1999P	Connecticut, MS	.25
1999D	Connecticut, MS	.25
1999S	Connecticut, PR	2.00
2000P	Massachusetts, MS	.25
2000D	Massachusetts, MS	.25
2000S	Massachusetts, PR	2.00
2000P	Maryland, MS	.25
2000D	Maryland, MS	.25
2000S	Maryland, PR	2.00
2000P	South Carolins, MS	.25
2000D	South Carolina, MS	.25
2000S	South Carolina, PR	2.00
2000P	New Hampshire, MS	.25
2000D	New Hampshire, MS	.25
2000S	New Hampshire, PR	2.00
2000P	Virginia, MS	.25
2000D	Virginia, MS	.25
2000S	Virginia, PR	2.00
2001P	New York, MS	.25
2001D	New York, MS	.25
2001S	New York, PR	2.00
2001P	North Carolina, MS	.25
2001D	North Carolina, MS	.25
2001S	North Carolina, PR	2.00

Rhode Island

Vermont

Indiana

Mississippi

Kentucky

Tennessee

Illinois

Alabama

Ohio

Louisiana

Maine

Missouri

Date and Mint Mark	Description	Buying Price
2001P	Rhode Island, MS	.25
2001D	Rhode Island, MS	.25
2001S	Rhode Island, PR	2.00
2001P	Vermont, MS	.25
2001D	Vermont, MS	.25
2001S	Vermont, PR	2.00
2001P	Kentucky, MS	.25
2001D	Kentucky, MS	.25
2001S	Kentucky, PR	2.00
2002P	Tennessee, MS	.25
2002D	Tennessee, MS	.25
2002S	Tennessee, PR	2.00
2002P	Ohio, MS	.25
2002D	Ohio, MS	.25
2002S	Ohio, PR	2.00
2002P	Louisiana, MS	.25
2002D	Louisiana, MS	.25
2002S	Louisiana, PR	2.00

Date and Mint Mark	Description	Buying Price
2002P	Indiana, MS	.25
2002D	Indiana, MS	.25
2002S	Indiana, PR	2.00
2002P	Mississippi, MS	.25
2002D	Mississippi, MS	.25
2002S	Mississippi, PR	2.00
2003P	Illinois, MS	.25
2003D	Illinois, MS	.25
2003S	Illinois, PR	2.00
2003P	Alabama, MS	.25
2003D	Alabama, MS	.25
2003S	Alabama, PR	2.00
2003P	Maine, MS	.25
2003D	Maine, MS	.25
2003S	Maine, PR	2.00
2003P	Missouri, MS	.25
2003D	Missouri, MS	.25
2003S	Missouri, PR	2.00

Arkansas

Michigan

California

Minnesota

Florida

Texas

Oregon

Kansas

Iowa

Wisconsin

West Virginia

Nevada

Date and Mint Mark	Description	Buying Price
2003P	Arkansas, MS	.25
2003D	Arkansas, MS	.25
2003S	Arkansas, PR	2.00
2004P	Michigan, MS	.25
2004D	Michigan, MS	.25
2004S	Michigan, PR	2.00
2004P	Florida, MS	.25
2004D	Florida, MS	.25
2004S	Florida, PR	2.00
2004P	Texas, MS	.25
2004D	Texas, MS	.25
2004S	Texas, PR	2.00
2004P	Iowa, MS	.25
2004D	Iowa, MS	.25
2004S	Iowa, PR	2.00
2004P	Wisconsin, MS	.25
2004D	Wisconsin, MS	.25
2004S	Wisconsin, PR	2.00

Date and Mint Mark	Description	Buying Price
2005P	California, MS	.25
2005D	California, MS	.25
2005S	California, PR	2.00
2005P	Minnesota, MS	.25
2005D	Minnesota, MS	.25
2005S	Minnesota, PR	2.00
2005P	Oregon, MS	.25
2005D	Oregon, MS	.25
2005S	Oregon, PR	2.00
2005P	Kansas, MS	.25
2005D	Kansas, MS	.25
2005S	Kansas, PR	2.00
2005P	West Virginia, MS	.25
2005D	West Virginia, MS	.25
2005S	West Virginia, PR	2.00
2006P	Nevada, MS	.25
2006D	Nevada, MS	.25
2006S	Nevada, PR	2.00

STATE QUARTERS (cont.)

Nebraska

Colorado

Idaho

Wyoming

North Dakota

South Dakota

Utah

Photo not available at press time

Alaska

Montana

Washington

Photo not available at press time

Hawaii

Photo not available at press time

Arizona

Date and Mint Mark	Description	Buying Price
2006P	Nebraska, MS	.25
2006D	Nebraska, MS	.25
2006S	Nebraska, PR	2.00
2006P	Colorado, MS	.25
2006D	Colorado, MS	.25
2006S	Colorado, PR	2.00
2006P	North Dakota, MS	.25
2006D	North Dakota, MS	.25
2006S	North Dakota, PR	2.00
2006P	South Dakota, MS	.25
2006D	South Dakota, MS	.25
2006S	South Dakota, PR	2.00
2007P	Montana, MS	.25
2007D	Montana, MS	.25
2007S	Montana, PR	2.00
2007P	Washington, MS	.25
2007D	Washington, MS	.25
2007S	Washington, PR	2.00

Date and Mint Mark	Description	Buying Price
2007P	Idaho, MS	.25
2007D	Idaho, MS	.25
2007S	Idaho, PR	2.00
2007P	Wyoming, MS	.25
2007D	Wyoming, MS	.25
2007S	Wyoming, PR	2.00
2007P	Utah, MS	.25
2007D	Utah, MS	.25
2007S	Utah, PR	2.00
2008P	Alaska, MS	.25
2008D	Alaska, MS	.25
2008S	Alaska, PR	2.00
2008P	Hawaii, MS	.25
2008D	Hawaii, MS	.25
2008S	Hawaii, PR	2.00
2008P	Arizona, MS	.25
2008D	Arizona, MS	.25
2008S	Arizona, PR	2.00

HALF DOLLARS
Flowing Hair

Date and Mint Mark	Buying Price
1794	1,200.00
1795	330.00

Draped Bust

Date and Mint Mark	Buying Price
1796 15 Stars	6,000.00
1796 16 Stars	6,000.00
1797 15 Stars	6,000.00
1801 to 1802	300.00
1803 to 1807	75.00

Capped Bust

Date and Mint Mark	Buying Price
1807	60.00
1808 to 1814	20.00
1815	425.00
1817 to 1836	20.00
1837 to 1839	20.00
1839O	100.00

Liberty Seated

Date and Mint Mark	Buying Price
1839 to 1852O	10.00
1850	100.00
1851	125.00
1852	125.00
1853O No Arrows	25,000.00
1853 to 1855	7.00
1855S Arrows	100.00
1856 to 1865S	6.00
1866 to 1873CC	6.00
1870CC	500.00
1871CC	100.00
1873 to 1874S	5.00
1875 to 1878	5.00
1878CC	50.00
1878S	3,500.00
1879 to 1890	100.00
1891	15.00

Barber

Date and Mint Mark	Buying Price
1892	6.00
1892O	100.00
1892S	75.00
1893 to 1897	4.00
1897O	55.00
1897S	55.00
1898 to 1915	4.00

Liberty Walking

Date and Mint Mark	Buying Price
1916 to 1920	3.35
1921	60.00
1921D	100.00
1923 to 1947	3.35

Franklin

Date and Mint Mark	Buying Price
1948 to 1964	3.35

Kennedy - Silver

Date and Mint Mark	Buying Price
1964	3.35

Kennedy - Silver Clad

Date and Mint Mark	Buying Price
1965 to 1970	2.00

Kennedy - Copper Clad

Date and Mint Mark	Buying Price
1971 to 2006	.50

SILVER DOLLARS

Flowing Hair

Date and Mint Mark	Buying Price
1794	15,000.00
1795	600.00

Draped Bust

Date and Mint Mark	Buying Price
1795	500.00
1796 to 1798	500.00
1798 to 1803	300.00

Note: Silver dollars must grade very good (VG) or better to command prices listed.

Liberty Seated

Date and Mint Mark	Buying Price
1840 to 1873	75.00
1851 and 1852	1,200.00
1854	450.00
1855	300.00
1858 Proofs only	1,000.00
1870CC	125.00
1870S	20,000.00
1871CC	1,000.00
1872CC	400.00
1872S	100.00
1873CC	1,600.00

Liberty Head

Date and Mint Mark	Buying Price
1878 to 1892	10.00
1878CC to 1881CC	35.00
1882CC to 1884CC	30.00
1885CC	165.00
1889CC	230.00
1893CC	100.00
1890O to 1893O	10.00
1893S	1,100.00
1894	450.00
1895	6,500.00
1895O	100.00
1895S	150.00
1896 to 1903	10.00
1903O	100.00
1904 to 1921	10.00

Peace

Date and Mint Mark	Buying Price
1921	7.00
1922 to 1927	6.70
1928	150.00
1928S to 1935S	6.70

Eisenhower

Date and Mint Mark	Buying Price
1971 to 1978	1.00

Susan B. Anthony

Date and Mint Mark	Buying Price
1979 to 1981	1.00

TRADE DOLLARS

Date and Mint Mark	Buying Price
1873 to 1878	45.00
1878CC	100.00
1879 to 1883	300.00

GOLD DOLLARS

Type 1 Liberty Head

Date and Mint Mark	Buying Price
1849 to 1854	70.00

Type 2 Indian Head, Small

Date and Mint Mark	Buying Price
1854 to 1855	110.00
1855C	450.00
1855D	1,600.00
1855O	165.00
1856S	300.00

IMPORTANT: Buying prices listed are for coins graded VF or better. Bent, damaged or badly worn coins are worth less.

Type 3 Indian Head, Large

Date and Mint Mark	Buying Price
1856 to 1889	75.00
1856D	1,100.00
1860D	840.00
1861D	2,000.00
1875	800.00

GOLD 2 ½ DOLLARS

Capped Bust Right

Date and Mint Mark	Buying Price
1796	6,000.00
1797 to 1807	1,500.00

Capped Bust Left

Date and Mint Mark	Buying Price
1808	6,000.00

Capped Head Left

Date and Mint Mark	Buying Price
1821 to 1827	1,500.00
1829 to 1833	1,700.00
1834 No Motto	3,000.00

Classic Head

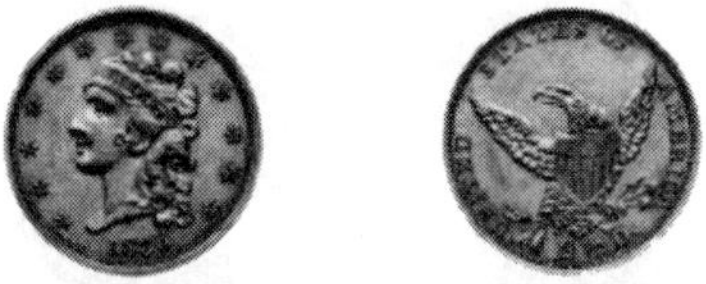

Date and Mint Mark	Buying Price
1834 to 1839	150.00

Coronet Head

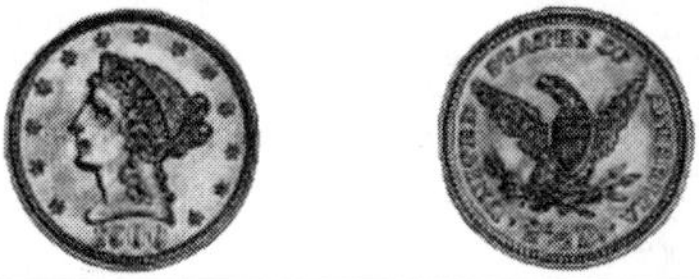

Date and Mint Mark	Buying Price
1840 to 1907	80.00
1848 California	4,000.00
1854D	1,000.00
1854S	15,000.00
1855D	750.00
1856D	2,300.00
1875	1,000.00

Indian Head

Date and Mint Mark	Buying Price
1908 to 1929	100.00
1911D	750.00

3 DOLLARS

Date and Mint Mark	Buying Price
1854 to 1873	350.00
1854D	2,900.00
1873 Closed 3	1,400.00
1880 to 1889	300.00

4 DOLLARS

Date and Mint Mark	Buying Price
1879 to 1880	22,000.00

GOLD 5 DOLLARS

Capped Bust - Small Eagle

Date and Mint Mark	Buying Price
1795	4,500.00
1798	10,000.00

Capped Bust - Heraldic Eagle

Date and Mint Mark	Buying Price
1795 to 1797	1,500.00
1798 to 1807	1,000.00

IMPORTANT: Buying prices listed are for coins graded VF or better. Bent, damaged or badly worn coins are worth less.

Capped Draped Bust Left

Date and Mint Mark	Buying Price
1807 to 1812	1,000.00

Capped Head

Date and Mint Mark	Buying Price
1813 to 1820	1,000.00
1815	10,000.00
1819	3,000.00
1821	3,000.00
1823	1,000.00
1824 to 1826	2,500.00
1829	8,000.00
1830 to 1834	5,500.00

Classic Head

Date and Mint Mark	Buying Price
1834 to 1838	150.00
1838C	750.00
1838D	600.00

Coronet Head

Date and Mint Mark	Buying Price
1839 to 1908	150.00
1842C Large Date	300.00
1842C Small Date	1,500.00
1854S	35,000.00
1861C	500.00
1861D	1,000.00
1864S	1,600.00
1865S	500.00
1870CC	1,800.00
1875	6,000.00
1878CC	1,000.00

Indian Head

Date and Mint Mark	Buying Price
1908 to 1916	150.00
1909O	600.00
1929	1,500.00

GOLD 10 DOLLARS

Capped Bust Right

Date and Mint Mark	Buying Price
Small Eagle, 1795 to 1797	5,500.00
Heraldic Eagle, 1797 to 1804	3,000.00

Coronet Head

Date and Mint Mark	Buying Price
1838 to 1907	350.00
1858	1,500.00
1859O	1,250.00
1859S	650.00
1863	1,200.00
1864S	1,500.00
1865S	1,900.00
1866S	950.00
1867S	600.00
1870CC	2,500.00
1871CC	800.00
1872	800.00
1872CC	1,000.00
1873	1,500.00
1873CC	2,000.00
1875	15,000.00
1875CC	1,500.00
1876	1,100.00
1876CC	900.00
1877	900.00
1877CC	900.00
1878CC	1,200.00
1879CC	3,000.00
1879O	700.00
1883O	1,100.00

$10 Indian Head

Date and Mint Mark	Buying Price
1907 to 1932	325.00
1920S	2,500.00
1930S	2,000.00
1933	25,000.00

GOLD $20 DOLLARS
Liberty

Date and Mint Mark	Buying Price
1850 to 1907	600.00
1854O	15,000.00
1855O	1,200.00
1856O	25,000.00
1859O	1,600.00
1860O	1,600.00
1861O	1,100.00
1866S	850.00
1870CC	35,000.00
1871CC	2,300.00
1872CC	700.00
1879O	2,400.00
1881	1,500.00
1882	2,800.00
1885	2,400.00
1886	3,000.00
1891	1,200.00
1891CC	1,200.00

$20 St. Gaudens

Date and Mint Mark	Buying Price
1907 MCMVII	2,400.00
1907 to 1916	600.00
1920S	4,300.00
1921	4,700.00
1922 to 1928	600.00
1927D	50,000.00
1927S	1,500.00
1929	2,000.00
1930 to 1932	3,000.00

GOLD COMMEMORATIVE COINS

Date and Mint Mark	Buying Price
1903 $1 Louisiana Purchase	150.00
1904-05 $1 Lewis & Clark Exposition	200.00
1915S $1 Panama-Pacific Exposition	150.00
1916 $1 McKinley Memorial	150.00
1917 $1 McKinley Memorial	175.00
1922 $1 Grant Memorial, With Star	450.00
1922 $1 Grant Memorial, Without Star	450.00
1915S $2.50 Panama-Pacific Exposition	550.00
1926 $2.50 Philadelphia Sesquicentennial	125.00
1984P and D $10 Olympic	300.00
1984S $10 Olympic	300.00
1984W $10 Olympic	300.00
1986W $5 Liberty	150.00
1987W $5 Constitution	150.00
1988W $5 Oylmpic	150.00
1989W $5 Congress	150.00
1991W $5 Mount Rushmore	150.00
1992W $5 Olympic	150.00
1992W $5 Columbus	150.00

Date and Mint Mark	Buying Price
1993W $5 Bill of Rights	150.00
1994W $5 World Cup	150.00
1995W $5 Civil War	250.00
1995W $5 Olympic Torch	200.00
1995W $5 Olympic Stadium	200.00
1995W $5 WWII	150.00
1996W $5 Flag Bearer	200.00
1996W $5 Cauldron	200.00
1996W $5 Smithsonian	300.00
1997W $5 F.D.R.	150.00
1997W $5 Jackie Robinson	800.00
1999W $5 George Washington	150.00
2000W $10 Library of Congress	400.00
2001W $5 Capitol Visitor Centre	200.00
2002W $5 Salt Lake City Olympics	150.00
2003W $10 First Flight	300.00
2006 $5 San Francisco Mint Museum	150.00
2007W $5 Jamestown	150.00

SILVER COMMEMORATIVE COINS

Date and Mint Mark	Buying Price
1982D or S 50¢ George Washington	2.00
1983P, D or S $1 Los Angeles Olympics	5.00
1984P, D or S, $1 Los Angeles Olympics	5.00
1986D or S 50¢ Statue of Liberty	2.00
1986P or S $1 Statue of Liberty	5.00
1987P or S $1 Constitution	5.00
1988D or S $1 Seoul Olympiad	5.00
1989D or S 50¢ Congress	2.00
1989D or S $1 Congress	8.00
1990W or P $1 Eisenhower	8.00
1991D $1 Korean War	6.00
1991D or S 50¢ Mount Rushmore	7.00
1991D or S $1 USO	6.00
1991P or S $1 Mount Rushmore	12.00
1992D or W $1 White House	10.00
1992D or S $1 XXV Olympiad	10.00
1992D or S 50¢ Christopher Columbus	4.00
1992D or P $1 Christopher Columbus	10.00
1992P or S 50¢ XXV Olympiad	3.00
1993D or W $1 D-Day	20.00
1993-1994P or S $1 Thomas Jefferson	10.00
1993W or S 50¢ Bill of Rights	5.00
1994D or P 50¢ World Cup	4.00
1994D or S $1 World Cup	15.00
1994D or S $1 U.S. Capitol	10.00
1994W or P $1 Vietnam Veterans Mem.	30.00
1994W or P $1 U.S. Prisoner of War Mem.	30.00
1994W or P $1 Women in Military	20.00
1995D $1 Olympics, Gymnastics	30.00
1995D $1 Olympics, Paralympic	30.00
1995D $1 Olympics, Track & Field	30.00
1995D $1 Olympics, Cycling	30.00
1995D or S $1 Bill of Rights	7.00
1995P 50¢ 50th Anniversary WWII	10.00
1995P or S $1 Civil War Battlefields	25.00
1995P $1 Cycling (PR)	15.00
1995P $1 Gymnastics (PR)	20.00
1995P $1 Paralympics (PR)	20.00
1995P $1 Track & Field (PR)	15.00
1995S 50¢ Civil War Battlefields	15.00
1995S 50¢ Olympics, Basketball	8.00
1995S 50¢ Olympics, Baseball	8.00
1995S 50¢ Olympics, Swimming	30.00
1995S 50¢ Olympics, Soccer	30.00
1995 W or P $1 Special Olympics	10.00
1996D $1 Olympics, Tennis	60.00
1996D $1 Olympics, Paralympic	100.00
1996D $1 Olympics, Rowing	100.00
1996D P $1 Olympics, Jump	100.00
1996D $1 Smithsonian (MS)	35.00
1996P $1 Smithsonian (PR)	15.00
1996P $1 High Jump	15.00
1996P $1 Paralympics (PR)	20.00
1996P $1 Rowing (PR)	20.00
1996P $1 Tennis (PR)	20.00
1996S $1 Community Service (MS)	75.00
1996S $1 Community Service (PR)	25.00
1997P $1 Botanic Gardens (MS & PR)	15.00
1997P $1 Law Enforcement (MS & PR)	50.00
1997S $1 Robinson (MS & PR)	20.00
1998S $1 Black Patriots (MS & PR)	50.00
1998S $1 Robert F. Kennedy (MS & PR)	15.00
1999P $1 Dolly Madison (MS & PR)	20.00
1999P $1 Yellowstone	20.00
2000P $1 Leif Ericson (MS & PR)	40.00
2000P $1 Library of Congress (MS & PR)	15.00
2001P or D $1 American Indian	150.00
2001P 50¢ U.S. Capitol (MS & PR)	5.00
2002P $1 Olympics, Salt Lake City (MS & PR)	15.00
2003P $1 First Flight (MS & PR)	15.00
2003P 50¢ First Flight (MS & PR)	5.00
2004P $1 Edison (MS & PR)	15.00
2004P $1 Lewis & Clark (MS & PR)	15.00
2005P $1 Chief Justice J. Marshall (MS & PR)	15.00
2005P $1 U.S. Marine Corps (MS & PR)	20.00
2006P $1 Benjamin Franklin, Signature	20.00
2006P $1 Benjamin Franklin, Kite	20.00
2006S $1 San Francisco Mint Museum	15.00
2007P $1 Jamestown	15.00

WORLD GOLD COINS

This partial listing of common world gold coins indicates the prices dealers are willing to pay based on the Canadian dollar gold price as at July 15th, 2007 ($672.00 U.S., 1.04 Can./U.S.). Prices will fluctuate with the market price of gold, and the Canadian-U.S. dollar exchange rate.

AUSTRIA

Date and Denom.	Fine Gold Content Oz.	Buying Price
1912 10K	0.0980	53.00
1915 20K	0.1960	106.00
1915 100K	0.9803	530.00
1915 1D	0.1109	61.00
1914 4D	0.4438	225.00
1892 10Fr	0.0933	51.00
1892 20Fr*	0.1867	102.00

BAHAMAS

Date and Denom.	Fine Gold Content Oz.	Buying Price
1967 $10	0.1177	64.00
1971 $10	0.1177	64.00
1972 $10	0.0940	51.00
1967 $20	0.2355	128.00
1971 $20*	0.2355	128.00
1972 $20	0.1880	103.00
1967 $50	0.5888	320.00
1971 $50	0.5888	320.00
1972 $50	0.4708	258.00
1967 $100	1.1776	645.00
1971 $100	1.1776	645.00
1972 $100	0.9420	516.00

BELGIUM

Date and Denom.	Fine Gold Content Oz.	Buying Price
1867 to 1914 20Fr	0.1867	102.00

BERMUDA

Date and Denom.	Fine Gold Content Oz.	Buying Price
1970 $20	0.2355	130.00
1977 $50	0.1172	64.00
1975 $100*	0.2304	126.00
1977 $100	0.2344	128.00

CAYMAN ISLANDS

Date and Denom.	Fine Gold Content Oz.	Buying Price
1972 $25*	0.2532	138.00
1974 $50	0.1823	100.00
1974 $100	0.3646	200.00
1975 $100	0.3646	200.00
1977 $100	0.3646	200.00

* Coin illustrated

CHILE

Date and Denom.	Fine Gold Content Oz.	Buying Price
1898 to 1900 5p	0.0883	48.00
1896 to 1901 10p*	0.1766	96.00
1896 to 1917 20p	0.3532	200.00
1926 to 1980 100p	0.5886	325.00

COLOMBIA

Date and Denom.	Fine Gold Content Oz.	Buying Price
1913 to 1929 2 ½ p	0.1177	64.00
1913 to 1930 5p	0.2355	128.00
1919 and 1924 10p	0.4710	255.00
1973 1500p*	0.5527	303.00

FRANCE

Date and Denom.	Fine Gold Content Oz.	Buying Price
1856 to 1869 5Fr	0.0467	26.00
1854 to 1914 10Fr	0.0933	52.00
1809 to 1914 20Fr*	0.1867	102.00
1810 to 1838 40Fr	0.3734	205.00
1855 to 1864 50Fr	0.4667	255.00
1855 to 1913 100Fr	0.9335	510.00

* Coin illustrated

GERMANY

Date and Denom.	Fine Gold Content Oz.	Buying Price
1872 to 1914 10DM	0.1152	63.00
1871 to 1914 20DM*	0.2304	125.00

GREAT BRITAIN

Date and Denom.	Fine Gold Content Oz.	Buying Price
1863 to 1915 ½ Sov.	0.1177	64.00
1871 to 1968 Sov.*	0.2354	128.00
1887 Two Pound	0.4708	256.00
1897 Two Pound	0.4708	256.00
1902 Two Pound	0.4708	256.00
1911 Two Pound	0.4708	256.00
1937 Two Pound	0.4708	256.00
1887 Five Pound	1.1773	645.00
1897 Five Pound	1.1773	645.00
1902 Five Pound	1.1773	645.00
1911 Five Pound	1.1773	645.00
1937 Five Pound	1.1773	645.00

IRAN

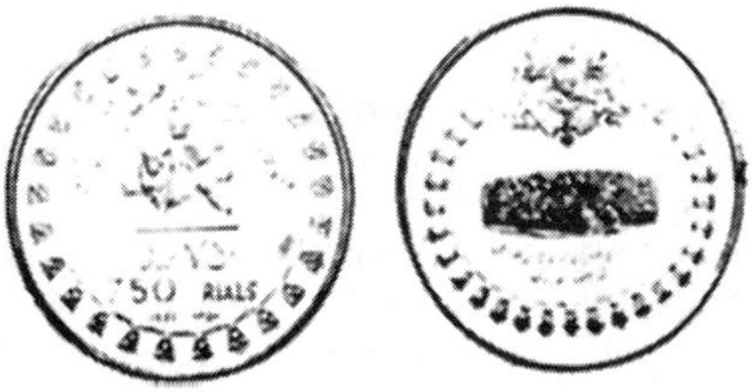

Date and Denom.	Fine Gold Content Oz.	Buying Price
1971 500R	0.1883	103.00
1971 750R*	0.2827	155.00
1971 1000R	0.3770	206.00
1971 2000R	0.7541	413.00

ITALY

Date and Denom.	Fine Gold Content Oz.	Buying Price
1932 to 1860 10L	0.0931	51.00
1831 to 1860 20L*	0.1867	103.00
1822 to 1831 40L	0.3733	205.00
1832 to 1844 100L	0.9332	510.00

JAMAICA

Date and Denom.	Fine Gold Content Oz.	Buying Price
1972 $20*	0.2531	140.00
1975, 1976 $100	0.2265	124.00
1978 $100	0.3281	180.00
1978, 1979 $250	1.2507	685.00

MEXICO

Date and Denom.	Fine Gold Content Oz.	Buying Price
1945 2p	0.0482	26.00
1945 2 1/2p	0.0602	33.00
1955 5p	0.1205	66.00
1959 10p*	0.2411	132.00
1959 20p	0.4823	265.00
1947 50p	1.2057	660.00

Above dates are restrikes.

NETHERLANDS

Date and Denom.	Fine Gold Content Oz.	Buying Price
1900 to 1937 1D*	0.1109	61.00
1912 5G	0.0973	53.00
1875 to 1933 10G	0.1947	107.00

PANAMA

Date and Denom.	Fine Gold Content Oz.	Buying Price
1975 to 1979 100B*	0.2361	129.00
1975 to 1979 500B	1.2067	661.00

RUSSIA

Date and Denom.	Fine Gold Content Oz.	Buying Price
1897 to 1911 5R*	0.1244	68.00
1897 7 1/2R	0.1867	102.00
1898 to 1911 10R	0.2489	136.00
1897 15R	0.3734	205.00
1977 to 1988 100R	0.5000	275.00

*Coin Illustrated

IMPORTANT: Buying prices listed are for coins graded VF or better. Bent, damaged or badly worn coins are worth less.

APPENDIX

BULLION VALUES

Silver and gold coins and other numismatic items are often bought by dealers for their bullion value, that is the value of the pure precious metals which they contain. The weight of precious metals is expressed in grams or troy ounces, not in avoirdupois ounces. A troy ounce is greater than an avoirdupois ounce.

1 Troy Ounce = 31.21035 Grams
1 Avoirdupois Ounce = 28.349 Grams

GOLD

The quantity of pure gold in gold coins is calculated by multiplying the gold fineness or purity of the coin by its weight in troy ounces or grams. Gold purity can also be expressed in karats, a 24-part system with 24-karats equalling pure gold, 22 karats equalling 22 parts gold to 2 parts base metal, 18 karats equalling 18 parts gold to 6 parts base metal etc.

Karats	Fineness	Purity
24	.999	99.9%
22	.916	91.6%
18	.750	75.0%
14	.585	58.5%
10	.417	41.7%
9	.375	37.5%

1 14-karat or .585 fine gold coin weighing 1 troy ounce contains 1 ounce x .585 = .585 troy ounces of pure gold. If gold is worth $600 per troy ounce, then this coin is worth $600 x .585 = $351. (See extended charts on following pages.)

SILVER

The quantity of pure silver in silver coins is calculated by multiplying the silver fineness or purity of the coin by its weight in troy ounces.

Description	Fineness	Purity
Pure	.9999	99.99%
Fine	.999	99.9%
Sterling	.925	92.5%
Coin	.800	80.0%
Coin	.500	50.0%

A .800 fine silver coin weighing 1 troy ounce contains 1 x .800 = .800 troy ounces of pure silver. If silver is worth $20 an ounce, then this coin is worth $20 x .800 = $16. (See extended charts on following pages.)

GOLD CONTENT OF CANADIAN GOLD COIN

Denom.	Date and Mint Mark	Gross Weigh (Grams)	Fineness	Pure Gold Content Grams	Troy Oz.
1 pd.	1908C-1910C	7.99	.917	7.32	.236
1 pd.	1911C-1919C	7.99	.917	7.32	.236
$2	1865-1888	3.33	.917	3.05	.100
$5	1912-1914	8.36	.900	7.52	.242
$10	1912-1914	16.72	.900	15.05	.484
$20	1967	18.27	.900	16.45	.529
$5 M.L.	1982 to date	3.11	.9999	3.11	.100
$10 M.L.	1982 to date	7.78	.9999	7.78	.250
$20 M.L.	1986 to date	15.57	.9999	15.57	.500
$50 M.L.	1979 to date	31.10	.999	31.10	1. 000
$100	1976 (Unc.)	13.33	.583	7.78	.250
$100	1976 (Proof)	16.96	.917	15.55	.499
$100	1977-1986	16.96	.917	15.55	.499
$100	1987 to 2003	13.33	.583	7.78	.250
$100	2004 to date	12.00	.583	7.00	.225
$150	2000 to date	11.84	.750	8.88	.285
$175	1992	16.97	.916	15.544	.500
$200	1990 to 2003	17.106	.916	15.669	.500
$200	2004 to date	16.00	.917	14.67	.472
$300	2002 to 2006 (large)	60.00	.583	34.98	1.125
$300	2004 to 2006 (small)	45.00	.583	26.23	.843
$350	1998 to 2003	38.05	.99999	38.05	1.223
$350	2004 to 2006	35.00	.99999	35.00	1.125

SILVER CONTENT OF CANADIAN SILVER COINS

Denom.	Date	Silver Content Fineness	Grams	Troy Oz.
$20	1985-1988	.925	31.103	1.000
$10	1973-1976	.925	44.955	1.445
$5	1973-1976	.925	22.477	.723
$5 M.L.	1987 to date	.999	31.103	1.000
$1	1935-1967	.800	18.661	.600
$1	1971 to date	.500	11.662	.375
50-cents	1870-1919	.925	10.792	.347
50-cents	1920-1967	.800	9.330	.300
25-cents	1870-1919	.925	5.370	.173
25-cents	1920-1967	.800	4.665	.150
25-cents	1967-1968	.500	2.923	.094
10-cents	1858-1919	.925	2.146	.069
10-cents	1920-1967	.800	1.866	.060
10-cents	1967-1968	.500	1.170	.038
5-cents	1858-1919	.925	1.080	.034
5-cents	1920-1921	.800	.933	.030

PLATINUM CONTENT OF CANADIAN PLATINUM COINS

Denom.	Date	Platinum Content Fineness	Grams	Troy Oz.
$300	1990-2004	.9999	31.1	1.000
$150	1990-2004	.9999	15.6	.500
$75	1990-2004	.9999	7.8	.250
$30	1990-2004	.9999	3.1	.100

BULLION VALUES OF CANADIAN GOLD COINS

Computed from $500 to $900 (Canadian dollars) per troy ounce in increments of $100 Canadian.

Denom.	Date and Mint Mark	$500	$600	$700	$800	$900
1 pd.	1908C-1910C	118.00	141.60	165.20	188.80	212.40
1 pd.	1911C-1919C	118.00	141.60	165.20	188.80	212.40
$2	1865-1888	50.00	60.00	70.00	80.00	90.00
$5	1912-1914	121.00	145.20	169.40	193.60	217.80
$10	1912-1914	242.00	290.40	338.80	387.20	435.60
$20	1967	264.50	317.40	370.30	423.20	476.10
$5 M.L.	1982 to date	50.00	60.00	70.00	80.00	90.00
$10 M.L.	1982 to date	125.00	150.00	175.00	200.00	225.00
$20 M.L.	1986 to date	250.00	300.00	350.00	400.00	450.00
$50 M.L.	1979 to date	500.00	600.00	700.00	800.00	900.00
$100	1976 (Unc)	125.00	150.00	175.00	200.00	225.00
$100	1976 (Proof)	250.00	300.00	350.00	400.00	450.00
$100	1977-1986	250.00	300.00	350.00	400.00	450.00
$100	1987 to 2003	125.00	150.00	175.00	200.00	225.00
$100	2004 to date	112.50	135.00	157.50	180.00	202.50
$150	1998 to date	142.50	171.00	200.00	228.00	256.50
$175	1992	250.00	300.00	350.00	400.00	450.00
$200	1990 to 2003	250.00	300.00	350.00	400.00	450.00
$200	2004 to date	236.00	283.20	330.40	377.60	424.80
$300	2002 to 2006 (large)	562.50	675.00	787.50	900.00	1,012.50
$300	2004 to 2006 (small)	421.95	506.35	590.75	675.15	759.50
$350	1998 to 2003	611.50	733.80	856.10	978.40	1,100.70
$350	2004 to 2006	562.65	675.16	787.70	900.20	1,012.75

BULLION VALUES OF CANADIAN SILVER COINS

Computed from $5 to $50 per troy ounce in increments of $10 Canadian.

Denom.	Fineness	$5	$10	$20	$30	$40	$50
$20	.925	5.00	10.00	20.00	30.00	40.00	50.00
$10	.925	7.23	14.00	28.90	43.35	57.80	72.15
$5	.925	3.62	7.23	14.46	21.69	28.92	36.15
$5 M.L.	.999	5.00	10.00	20.00	30.00	40.00	50.00
$1	.800	3.00	6.00	12.00	18.00	24.00	30.00
$1	.500	1.88	3.75	7.50	11.25	15.00	18.75
50 cents	.925	1.74	3.47	6.94	10.41	13.88	17.35
50 cents	.800	1.50	3.00	6.00	9.00	12.00	15.00
25 cents	.925	.87	1.73	3.46	5.19	6.92	8.65
25 cents	.800	.75	1.50	3.00	4.50	6.00	7.50
25 cents	.500	.47	.94	1.88	2.82	3.76	4.70
10 cents	.925	.35	.69	1.38	2.07	2.76	3.45
10 cents	.800	.30	.60	1.20	1.80	2.40	3.00
10 cents	.500	.19	.38	.76	1.14	1.52	1.90
5 cents	.925	.17	.34	.68	1.02	1.36	1.70
5 cents	.800	.15	.30	.60	.90	1.20	1.50

Sat 10, 5.
Sun 10 to 3
Airport Hilton

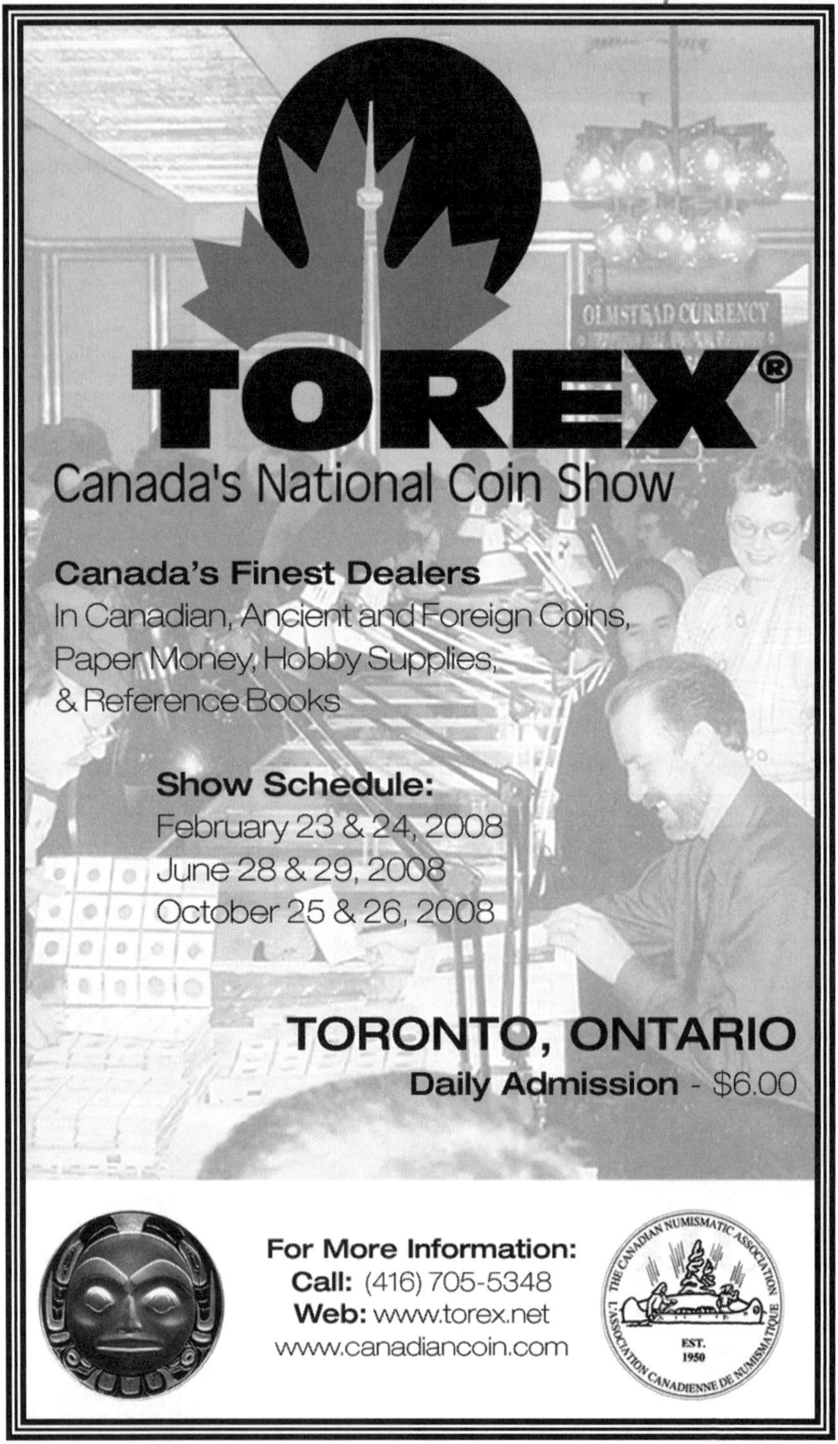